The Road to Duchesne

By
Mica Boyd Johnston

Table of Contents

Dedication

To my children,

Sunny, Russell, Danny, Nicole and Steven.

May you always know where you came from, even as you chase your own roads.

With all my love.

Page Blank Intentionally

Chapter 1: Change of Scenery

My eyes were closed as I rested my head on the open car window. Warm air blew across my face as we drove through the hot, dry Mojave Desert. Occasionally, my long hair would whirl in the wind and tickle my face, prompting me to brush it away. Sweat dripped from every pore, and my arm clung to the sticky leather seat of the station wagon, making it impossible to move without a faint sucking sound. The heat pressed down, intensifying the discomfort as the sun baked the interior, turning the seat into a tacky, unforgiving surface that held me in place.

I drifted in and out of sleep as the miles went by while replaying memories of the past summer and all the events that had taken place in just a short time—core memories that would last a lifetime. Exhaustion weighed on me, both mentally and physically, and the oppressive heat only added to my drowsiness, pulling me into a haze of sleepiness. I spent the last few days uncertain about what to expect next. Unsure about our life going forward. Uncertainty was a cruel and relentless part of life, especially through the eyes of a child. It lingers like a shadow, casting doubt and fear over even the simplest of moments. Every decision made by my parents felt daunting and vast, almost insurmountable. I could only hope they knew what they were doing.

Over the last few months, our family had been uprooted from the bustling, sun-soaked streets of Los Angeles to the quiet, isolated farmlands of central California. The move was a cultural shock that hit me like a tidal wave. I went from the familiarity of city life—friends, family, and the comforting chaos of urban living—to the eerie silence of vast, empty fields that seemed to stretch on forever. It was as if I had been dropped into another world, one where everything moved slower, where the air smelled of earth and crops instead of concrete and exhaust fumes. We left our family and friends knowing that I may never see any of them again.

Just as I began to adjust to the new rhythms of farm life, tragedy struck. My loyal, loving dog, Brownie, who had been my only constant through the turmoil, suddenly passed away. Brownie was more than just a pet; he was my confidant, the one friend who made the loneliness bearable. His death left a gaping hole in my heart, a wound that felt too deep to heal. I remember lying on my bed, feeling like the whole world had crumbled around me. The sadness was overwhelming, a suffocating weight that a 10-year-old shouldn't have to bear.

Plus, Dad had delivered the news that we were moving again—this time to Texas. The thought of starting over once more, just as I had lost Brownie, was almost too much to process. It was a double whammy, a one-two punch of loss and upheaval that left me feeling like I was being tossed around in a storm with no end in sight.

We left California on a late summer morning, the sun casting long, golden shadows as we packed up the last of our things and set out on what Dad called our "new adventure" to Texas. The air was thick with the scent of goodbye, and as we drove away, I watched the familiar landscape fade in the rearview mirror, my heart heavy with the weight of leaving Brownie behind. Dad's new job had become the compass that now steered our lives, pulling us toward an unknown future.

As I lay there with my head on the open window seal, drifting in and out of slumber, my thoughts drifted away from Brownie and now focused on Texas. I didn't know much about Texas, only what I had seen in old Westerns. I grew up watching John Wayne and Clint Eastwood, their larger-than-life personas filling our living room with tales of dusty trails and rugged cowboys. The idea of Texas sparked something in me—a flicker of excitement amidst the sadness. I imagined a place where the Wild West still lingered, where I might see a horse and buggy rolling down a dusty street or a real-live cowboy wearing a 10-gallon hat. I pictured myself standing on the edge of a rugged peak, the vast, arid landscape stretching out before me, raw and untamed. I wanted to feel the heat of the desert sun on my skin, see towering cacti and scurrying lizards, and soak in the raw power of wide-open spaces that seemed to go on forever.

In my half-conscious state, I think of the blazing Texas sun, and I can feel the heat wrap around me like a heavy blanket. The heat grows more intense, almost suffocating. My head shifts slightly on the window, and I suddenly realize that this isn't the Texas heat I am feeling. It's the scorching Mojave Desert sun beating down on my face, turning my dream into a sweltering nightmare. Dream and reality blur for the tiniest moment as I turn my face away from the window and face the inside of the station wagon. The inside of the car feels almost cooler, as if I had escaped the sun's relentless grasp.

Not feeling the beating desert sun on my face allowed me to drift back to my dreams, looking for relief from the heat, sadness, and uncertainty. Where was the happiness that I felt not so long ago? The bike rides through the tree-lined streets? The ice cream shop on the corner where all of us neighborhood kids would meet around 2 o'clock every summer day? The camping trips every year to Lake Castaic? Those memories seem so very far away, just out of reach. Then, my dream shifted to new possibilities. Maybe there were tree-lined streets in Texas? Maybe there was an ice cream shop on the corner that I could go to and find new friends. Maybe there were lakes in Texas where the family could go camping. Maybe, and I mean just maybe, the rest of the family could move to Texas, and all would be right again. The excitement started building deep in my soul.

I knew these thoughts could be reality. These thoughts were not out of reach, and now I felt that needed spark. But then my mind shifted to all the movies I had watched about Texas. There were no ice cream shops in the Wild West. I never saw family camping trips in any of the movies. Any trips taken in the movies ended up in a battle with some Indians. But I had seen lakes in the movies. But those lakes were few and far between and were primarily used for watering horses. I do vaguely remember a John Wayne movie where a bunch of brothers jumped into a lake and were having a great time, but that ended up in a shoot-out with some other guys. It was almost as if you had any fun in Texas; there were consequences.

I knew in my dream that I was looking for a spark of excitement to pull me out of the sadness that engulfed my soul. As a child, you live in the here and now, and I was hoping that once I felt that spark of excitement, all the world would be right again. I believed that just one moment of joy could chase away the shadows, that a new adventure could make everything better, and could make me forget the sadness that weighed so heavily on my heart. I clung to the hope that Texas would be that spark, that once I found it, everything would fall into place, and the pain of leaving California, of losing Brownie, would finally start to fade. But the fear and uncertainty lingered like a shadow that followed me no matter how fast I tried to run from it. As I drifted in and out of sleep, the image of Brownie kept returning. In my mind, he was still with me, sitting in the backseat just like he always did—his tail wagging with that endless enthusiasm, his eyes sparkling with that familiar, unconditional love. I could almost feel the softness of his fur as he nudged his head under my hand, the way he always sought comfort as much as he gave it.

In this dreamland, Brownie and I were inseparable, his head hanging out the window beside mine, both of us savoring the freedom of the open road. But then I'd wake up, the warmth of the wind on my face turning cold as I remembered he wasn't there. The backseat was empty, and the silence was deafening. The memory of him was like a knife twisting in my chest, a sharp, unrelenting reminder of everything I had lost. As much as I wanted to embrace this new adventure, a part of me felt hollow, like a piece of my heart had been left behind in California, buried with Brownie under the oak tree in Grandma's backyard. It was as if that tree held not just Brownie but all the love and laughter we had shared, now locked away in a place I could never visit again. I longed to be with him, to have just one more moment where everything felt right. Instead, I was left with a painful emptiness, a void that Texas could never fill, no matter how wide its skies or how wild its landscapes.

I'm not sure how long I slept. I would have slept all the way to Texas if it wasn't for Dad's booming voice piercing my sleep. I heard Dad tell Mom in his usual deep booming Viking voice – a voice so powerful it could cut through the loudest of noise or penetrate the deepest of sleeps, "We're coming up on the California state line." It was the kind of voice that could carry over the roar of a storm or through the haze of dreamland, leaving no doubt that he was speaking. At first, his words were mumbled, but as I regained full consciousness, I heard him say with purpose, "I need to call Murphy." Murphy was Dad's boss, a gruff, hardworking Irishman from Pennsylvania who now lived in West Texas. Like Dad, you could trust every word he said—no lies, no hidden meanings. Dad always said, "What good are words if everybody lies?" Dad always had some aphorism. We met Murphy once while we were still at Grandma's. Murphy had driven from L.A. all the way to Earlimart. He was so eager for Dad to work with him that he drove all the way over the Grapevine to make it happen.

Crossing the Grapevine during the 1970s was an especially daunting task, particularly when traveling on the old Highway 99. This notorious stretch of road connected Southern California to the rest of California, winding through the rugged Tehachapi Mountains with steep inclines and perilous sharp curves that tested even the most experienced drivers.

Back then, the Grapevine was infamous for its unpredictability. The narrow lanes of Highway 99 left little room for error, and with no modern safety features like today's wider lanes and guardrails, every twist and turn carried a heightened sense of danger. The road was often choked with traffic, including countless commercial trucks struggling to navigate the steep grades and tight curves. These trucks, burdened by heavy loads, frequently faced brake failures and overheating engines, leading to deadly accidents that could block the road for hours, leaving travelers stranded with no help for miles around.

Summer added another layer of difficulty. Temperatures on the Grapevine often soared above 100 degrees, turning the narrow, sunbaked highway into a treacherous gauntlet. Vehicles were prone to overheating, and there were few places, if any, to pull over safely. With no air conditioning in many cars and sparse services along the route, a breakdown could quickly become a dangerous situation, especially for families traveling with children.

Wind gusts were another constant threat, particularly for high-profile vehicles like big trucks and RVs. The narrow lanes and lack of barriers meant that strong winds could easily push cars off course, sometimes with disastrous results. Drivers had to fight to keep their cars steady, all while navigating the relentless curves and steep drops of the mountain pass.

I remember one trip we took over the Grapevine. We were following my dad's brother, my Uncle Jimmy. Uncle Jimmy was moving back to Bakersfield. I don't remember why, and I probably didn't care either, but I do remember his car was not in the best of shape. Dad had advised Uncle Jimmy many times about driving that "hotrod" over the Grapevine. Uncle Jimmy was a dirt track enthusiast. He owned many cars that were used on the local Dirt Track circuits in California. Uncle Jimmy told Dad that he wasn't leaving this particular hotrod behind and needed his help to get over the Grapevine. We managed to make the trip up through the mountain overpass with no problem, but as we were coming down the mountain, Uncle Jimmy's hotrod overheated.

He had no choice but to pull over in a narrow embankment and look under the hood. We pulled up behind him in the station wagon with Dad yelling at Mom, "Stay in the car! Do not let the kids out; it's too dangerous!" The scorching heat had no mercy back then. It felt like we were baking alive. I'm sure Dad and Uncle Jimmy felt worse in the hot sun with the hood up on Uncle Jimmy's car. We watched as Dad and Uncle Jimmy kept looking out from under the hood to make sure the traffic stayed in their lane. They were talking, and if body language said anything, Uncle Jimmy was mad as hell. Arms flailing up and down. Then Dad was angry, poking Uncle Jimmy in the chest and pointing at us in the car. Just then, all that anger fell away as a big rig came barreling down the mountain overpass with horn blaring. Later, Dad said the truck brakes had locked up, and the truck driver didn't have a whole lot of choices when that happened. When that big rig passed us within less than an inch, my heart stopped. The wind and heat from the truck consumed the entire station wagon.

The noise from the horn was deafening. Dad and Uncle Jimmy jumped out of the way as the big rig scraped the hot rod from rear to front. The truck driver was doing his best to control the truck, but as he finished around the curve, the wind caught him, and the truck went over on its side. The truck took out a couple of other cars that were headed down the hill. The truck came to a sliding stop about 100 yards from where we were. Dad and Uncle Jimmy went running towards the pile-up, trying to get people out of the cars. The truck driver climbed out of the side window, wiping his brow, glad to be alive. My heart was racing, and my little brother Michael was crying for Dad. My little sister Mia had jumped in the front seat and was on Mom's lap, crying. That day became a core memory, burned into my mind. Every time I had to cross the Grapevine after that, I'd feel a knot of anxiety in my stomach, the memory of that near-miss haunting me. The Grapevine wasn't just a road anymore—it was a reminder of how close we came to disaster and how lucky we were to make it out alive.

Crossing the Grapevine on Highway 99 back in the 70s was a test of skill, endurance, and nerve. It was a journey that required full attention and a level head. So, if Murphy was willing to brave the Grapevine just to talk to Dad about a job, it was clear how much he must have wanted him on his team. Only someone who truly understood Dad's value would tackle that treacherous stretch of road, knowing full well the risks involved. Murphy's willingness to cross the Grapevine said it all—he wasn't just offering Dad a job; he was showing just how far he'd go to get him on board. Years later, when I was a teenager, we would visit Murphy at his home in Midland, Texas. We spoke about his desire to get Dad on board, which was so strong he was willing to cross the Grapevine. Murphy, with his dry sense of humor, stated, "What's the Grapevine?" It would become a family story that is still passed around today. Murphy drove over the Grapevine, not knowing how dangerous the trip was. He just liked Dad and wanted him to come to work for him. Thirty years later, they were still working together.

Murphy was about as tall as my dad. A good 6'1 with a booming voice like Dad's. He had dark red hair, and his skin looked like leather. He was older than my dad by at least ten years, if I had to guess. While listening to Dad and Mom talk during the drive, I learned Murphy was married with two kids. His family lived in Midland, Texas, and he was headed there by airplane when we traveled to Texas. Murphy was the "Company Man." He was the one who told the work crews where to go. Murphy was the one who told Dad and his new crew to go to Houston, Texas. It was 1974, and a great oil boom was happening, and they needed Dad and his crew to get there ASAP. Murphy told Dad, "You're going to like Houston! It's a lot like L.A. but without all the hippies." I was comforted by the thought that Houston was like L.A., a place I dearly missed. However, I didn't understand why Murphy believed my dad had an aversion to hippies. After all, my Aunt Doodle, my mom's sister, was a hippie, and Dad liked her. Murphy's statement about Houston seemed to seal the deal for Dad. A handshake between the two men in my grandma's kitchen now meant we would soon be headed to Texas.

The road from Bakersfield to Blythe was long, slow, and hot. It felt like we were never going to get anywhere as slowly as we were driving. We finally arrived in Blythe and pulled over at an old gas station. Dad got out to use the pay phone. There were no cell phones back then. No email or text messaging either. So, every few miles, Dad would stop at a gas station to use the pay phone to call Murphy and check in. Dad would keep Murphy updated on our location, the distance we had covered, and the status of all the trucks. Murphy was concerned about the company trucks all the time. Apparently, those trucks were "worth a fortune," in Dad's words. Murphy was also

8

concerned about the crew. Whenever they traveled, they would inevitably lose a crew member or two along the way. Traveling for work and constantly moving is no easy task. It's a life that demands sacrifices, not just from the person on the road but from everyone connected to them. Some men managed to bring their immediate families along, but that didn't make it any easier. They left behind brothers, sisters, mothers, and fathers—people they'd grown up with and homes they'd known their entire lives. The familiarity of their surroundings and the comfort of lifelong connections all had to be abandoned for the uncertainty of a new place, a new job.

The emotional toll of uprooting yourself over and over again, of saying goodbye to everything familiar, can wear a person down. It's not just the physical act of packing up and leaving; it's the constant longing for what's been left behind. Every move meant starting over, forging new connections, and trying to build a sense of home in a place that never quite feels like it. The road might lead to new opportunities, but it's also paved with the sacrifices of leaving behind the people and places that made you who you are. Murphy knew this all too well. He had been moving from place to place his entire life. He had uprooted his wife and kids numerous times, so he made Dad aware of his responsibility of keeping the crew intact all the way to Texas.

Dad's crew operated eight Seismic Vibrator trucks. These trucks were huge and had a platform underneath, and when activated, the platform would lower down to the ground and lift the truck off its tires. Then, the platform would emit low-frequency vibrations into the Earth. On the open road, these trucks could travel about 45 mph, so from Bakersfield, California, to Houston, Texas, it should take about a week, including stops for gas and hotels. The route had to be mapped out exactly because there were only a few truck stops along the way. It was nothing like what we have today along the interstate highway system. Back then, you stopped at specific locations. These locations provided a bathroom break and maybe an area to stretch your legs. There were no huge truck stops where you could choose from a wide variety of food and drinks and have access to a bathroom with ten stalls. Nope, we only had small mom-and-pop gas stations with one bathroom that everyone had to take turns using. And none of the small gas stations provided food of any kind. We had to bring the food with us.

I can honestly say that I was raised on warm sandwiches, hot Coke, and the occasional McDonald's. God, how I loved McDonald's! Later on, as our travels continued, we did stop at a truck stop. One of the few in the country at the time. It became one of Dad's favorite stops. It was in El Paso, Texas, and there was a huge orange ball in the sky that you could see miles away. The huge orange ball had the number 76 written on it. At this truck stop, you could buy sodas and sandwiches and use a bathroom that was just for women and children. But going inside always raised my anxiety. Mom would make us all hold hands while walking to the bathrooms, and we all had to be in one stall. Mom did not trust the truck drivers and was always worried she would lose one of us kids. So even though we got to stop at a huge truck stop, which was exciting in itself, Mom made us all anxious with her worry. We did get to buy cold soft drinks and the occasional candy bar, though, which made the stop worth it.

Each one of the Seismic Vibrator trucks had a driver, and each driver had a family member who was following along in their car, station wagon, truck, or RV. All the drivers were men in those days, so all the wives and girlfriends would follow behind in their cars. Cars are fully loaded with all their kids and belongings. It was a real convoy, and my dad oversaw the whole crew. Our crew was called Crew #1129, and it was written on the side of every Vibrator truck. There were at least 30 people at any given time, including all the drivers, their families, and us. Half of those 30 people were kids. It was nice to have other kids around again, even if we only got to see each other when we stopped for fuel or to grab sandwich stuff at a grocery store.

When we left Grandma's house, I was incredibly sad and depressed about my dog Brownie. Dad said I could bring Brownie with us to Texas, but Brownie died the day before we were leaving. As the miles put us farther and farther away from Grandma's, the pain of losing Brownie was slowly subsiding. It hadn't disappeared, though, but having other kids around made me forget, if only for a while. Since we had arrived at Grandma's, I hadn't played with other kids all summer. Having someone to play with would be great, and I couldn't wait until we got to Texas so I could interact with these other kids. We got to hang out and play during bathroom stops at the gas station, but that never lasted long. A couple of the kids had bikes, and I was excited about that because we had to leave our bikes at Grandma's. Dad said there was no room for anything except necessities, which meant no bikes.

As I sat in the back seat of our station wagon with no AC, sweating, hot, and thirsty from the desert heat, I could see Dad walking back from the pay phone. Dad was a tall, blonde-haired Viking descendant who commanded respect wherever he went. My grandma would tell us stories about our Viking ancestry all the time. Honestly, I couldn't care less when I was a kid, but she ensured each of her grandkids knew their ancestry. After my grandma's stories, my mom always whispered with an added shrug, "We're Scotch-Irish." Either way, I didn't know what any of that meant, and I didn't care at the time. Later in life, it would be the driving force in my research of our Ancestry. Over the course of 30 years, my research proved Grandma had been right. But so had Mom.

Even with all the stories my grandmother told, I already knew that my dad was one of the strongest and most honest men I had ever met. When he said, "No," you did not ask again. He spoke with a firmness that made most people fearful but also made them know he was a man who meant what he said. Maybe it was because I was a child, but I always knew what was expected of me and how I should act wherever we were, because of my dad. In those days, my dad was the epitome of fun—at least, that's what we kids believed. On the other hand, my mom didn't share our enthusiasm, especially not when Dad would race down rural roads at speeds topping 80 mph with us kids in tow.

To me, it was thrilling! Nor did she approve of Dad's Fourth of July tradition of letting us kids ignite our own fireworks. I, however, found it exhilarating! And she certainly wasn't fond of the times Dad would sit us on his lap and let us steer the car. Yet, for us kids, it was an absolute blast! As time went on, Dad lost that spark of fun. Whether it was the constant moving or his taxing job that wore him down, I'm not certain. Perhaps he was simply exhausted, but by my teenage years, the fun-loving dad I once knew had faded.

I can remember one time when Uncle Jimmy, Aunt Peggy, and their four kids were following us from Bakersfield to Grandma's house in Earlimart. In our station wagon was me, my brother, my sister, and Mom and Dad, with Dad driving, of course.

We were almost at Grandma's house, the excitement of arriving hanging in the air, as the car rolled toward Deer Creek Bridge. It was a narrow crossing, barely wide enough for two cars to squeeze past each other. Just as we approached, Uncle Jimmy roared up beside Dad, his hot rod snarling like a wild beast. The challenge was unmistakable. He revved his engine, daring Dad to race.

Mom's voice cracked the tension, sharp and frantic. "No, Sonny! The kids are in the car, and we're too close to the bridge!" But Dad wasn't hearing her—his attention was locked with Uncle Jimmy's. Both men grinned, their engines growling in a back-and-forth symphony of rebellion. Each edged forward by mere inches, taunting the other, daring to see who'd make the first bold move.

And then, Uncle Jimmy hit the gas. His car surged ahead, tires screaming against the asphalt. Dad's jaw tightened, his grin widening like a kid on a carnival ride. He slammed the pedal to the floor, our car surging forward to catch up. The speedometer climbed, 50, 60, 70… 80 mph on a winding country road that was narrowing by the second. The bridge loomed ahead, a choke point of fate. One misstep and everything—everything could go up in flames.

In the other car, Aunt Peggy's arms flailed as she yelled at Uncle Jimmy. Mom was no quieter, her voice breaking into tears as she pleaded with Dad. "Sonny, stop! Stop! The kids! You can't both make it! Please!"

But the roar of the engines drowned out everything. Dad and Uncle Jimmy were locked in their own private universe, grins plastered across their faces, adrenaline coursing through their veins. The road blurred. The bridge rushed toward us. The tension was so thick it felt like the world might snap in two.

And then, everything slowed. The bridge, impossibly close, stretched out like an endless runway. I could see the concrete railing beside us, so near that I could reach out and touch it, feel its blistering heat. The chaos in the car faded into a muffled hum. Mom's screams, the kids' cries, the thunder of engines—they all seemed distant, like sounds from another world.

I watched it all unfold with a strange calm. The other kids' faces were streaked with terror; their mouths open in cries I could barely hear. The women clutched us tightly, their tears mixing with their frantic words. But Dad and Uncle Jimmy? They were alive in a way I'd never seen—lost in the thrill of the moment, grinning like they'd conquered the gods.

And then, it was over. We shot across the bridge, both cars intact, as if by some miracle. The world slammed back into focus. Mom's screams hit my ears like a crashing wave. The engines slowed, the hot leather seats creaked as we shifted back into place, and the suffocating tension eased.

As we rolled into Grandma's driveway, the cars barely stopped before everyone spilled out, voices exploding in fury and relief. Aunt Peggy let loose on Uncle Jimmy, while Mom turned her anger and tears on Dad. The kids clung to each other, sobbing in the summer heat.

But me? I stayed quiet. Deep down, I couldn't shake the rush. The thrill of it all. The danger. The excitement. It left a spark in me I couldn't admit—not to Mom, not to Aunt Peggy, not to anyone.

After the shouting died down and the adults disappeared inside, I lingered by Uncle Jimmy's car. The hood was hot to the touch, still humming with the energy of what had just happened. I placed my hand on it, feeling the heat seep into my palm.

"Get in the house!" Mom's voice snapped me out of my thoughts, and just like that, the moment was gone.

But it stayed with me. That day, I discovered something about Dad—and about myself. From then on, I called him "Fun Dad." And that wild, reckless drive over Deer Creek Bridge became a memory I'd hold onto forever, burning as brightly as the sun on that hot summer day

After Dad made the call to Murphy, he approached Mom with a smile. "Guess where we're going, Millie!" he exclaimed, using her nickname. Mom saw his smile and returned it, thinking he was joking around. But that wasn't the case. She said triumphantly, "We're going to Houston, Texas." Dad said excitedly, "Nope!" "We're headed to Utah!" Mom's smile faded into a look of confusion and a furrowed brow. I was also confused. "Utah?" she asked quietly as Dad walked past her, headed to let the rest of the crew know. I half-expected her to say, "Nope! Take me home, Sonny!" or "I'm done… let's go back home," or even her favorite, "This is for the birds." But she didn't say any of those things. Instead, she opened the passenger side door, slid into her seat, and stared out the window. "What did he mean we were going to Utah?" she mumbled. Mom looked puzzled yet delighted.

Mom was always the voice of reason when we were kids. Initially, I had hoped she would talk Dad into not leaving L.A., but for some reason, she never did. Perhaps the allure of an adventure sparked excitement within her. Considering it was 1974, a time when my mom didn't drive, didn't know how to write a check or pay a bill, and couldn't have a credit card, the prospect of a new environment might have offered her a sense of solace beyond her role as our mother. The idea of travel could have been her personal slice of excitement, a welcome change from her everyday existence. Maybe she was looking for a hint of joy in all this.

Mom was the youngest of 13 children. Mom also had a fraternal twin who died during childbirth, so all the older siblings felt they had a responsibility to watch over Mom. They affectionately called her Tiny. She was premature and so very small when she was born in the hills of Arkansas during the late 1930s. Everyone in the country was struggling from the Depression, and Mom's family was no different. All of her brothers worked in the Civilian Conservation Corps in Arkansas during the Depression. The Civilian Conservation Corps were work camps designed by the government to provide jobs for unemployed men to help families during the Depression. Mom came from a very proud family background whose ancestors worked hard for everything they had. The family did not take handouts. They helped each other and themselves. During the depression, my Mom's Dad, my grandfather, decided that it was time to move to California to ensure that his children survived and had better opportunities. So, the whole family, with the exception of my Aunt Annabelle, moved to Los Angeles. Mom's family was extremely close-knit, always spending time together and providing a strong support system for one another. But now, she was far from her brothers, sisters, and all those family members who had always looked after her. The thought that she might never see some of them again because of this move must have weighed heavily on her mind.

Just when we were becoming accustomed to the idea of moving to Texas, an unexpected turn of events sent us in an entirely different direction. This would be the first of many such instances. Over the next few years, this pattern would become all too familiar—being told we were going one way, only to end up somewhere completely different. Each new destination came with its own set of expectations, and as a child, those expectations were often my only anchor in the sea of constant change.

However, I quickly learned that expectations rarely matched reality. The places I had imagined, based on books or TV, were never quite what I encountered when we arrived. Those glossy images of perfect towns and friendly people didn't reflect the real world. While every place had its own unique quirks, fitting into each of them was anything but simple. You had to quickly adapt to the political beliefs and preferences of the community. I became quite skilled at reinventing myself over and over just to fit in.

Eventually, we all learned to brace ourselves as soon as Dad said, "You'll never guess where we are going." My mom would let out a slight moan, already dreading the upheaval, while Dad, ever the optimist, would joke, "I can hear your eyes rolling," every time our plans changed. But behind his jokes, and over time, I could sense the strain the constant moving put on him, too. He carried the weight of our collective uncertainty, and though he tried to make each new destination sound like an adventure, I could see the worry in his eyes.

Texas would be on the back burner for now. We were bound for a place I had never heard of: Duchesne, Utah. The name felt strange on my tongue, foreign and unfamiliar. I had no idea what to expect—no images of cowboys or vast deserts filled my mind, just a blank slate that only added to my growing anxiety. As a child, change was hard. Each move felt like tearing out a piece of myself and leaving it behind, and with every new destination, I was left trying to fill that void with new experiences and new people who never seemed to fit quite right.

The thought of starting over in yet another unknown place weighed heavily on me. I longed for stability, for a place where I could finally put down roots and not have to say goodbye to friends before I even had the chance to really know them. But as much as I wished for that, I knew better than to get my hopes up. Duchesne, Utah, was just the next stop in a journey that seemed to have no end, and all I could do was try to adjust to whatever came next, even as a part of me remained stuck in the past, clinging to the places and people we'd left behind.

I watched as all the men got out of their trucks and walked towards Dad. The old gas station, a relic from another era, had a weathered picnic table that now served as a makeshift platform for Dad's trusty, timeworn map. Faded signs and peeling paint hinted at a time when this place bustled with travelers, but now it stood as a quiet witness to our uncertain journey. The crew gathered around the map, deliberating over the new destination. Some of the men shifted uneasily, their discontent visible in the tense lines of their bodies—a silent testament to their reluctance to move to the new location. Most of the men and their families had accepted the move to Houston after a pep talk, but now, it looked as though Dad was going to have to give the pep talk of his life.

Dad faced the daunting task of assuring the crew that Utah would be a favorable stop, all the while remembering Murphy's caution about the potential loss of crew members. I could see the determination in Dad's eyes as he tried to rally the crew and maintain unity, but I could also see how the strain of leadership was weighing on him. After what seemed like an eternity, the decision was made: they would stay the night in Blythe and get a fresh start in the morning. The men needed to discuss the situation with their wives, and Dad needed to map out a new route.

I didn't mind the delay—it was too hot to even breathe in the car with no AC. Hopefully, the motel we'd stay at would have air conditioning or maybe even a pool where the kids could cool off. Mom hadn't said much, only letting out a few weary moans as she fanned herself with a tattered magazine. Her face was beet red, a clear sign of the heat and of her exhaustion. Her mind seemed elsewhere, likely preoccupied with thoughts of Utah. I'm sure she had no idea about Utah, just like the rest of us, and was left wondering what was in store for our little family there.

Dad approached the gas station attendant, asking if there were any motels nearby that could accommodate such a large crew. The attendant, an older man with grease-stained hands, pulled out a dusty, oversized phone book and flipped to the motel section. After Dad explained our situation, the attendant offered him the use of the station's rotary phone. Dad made a few calls and managed to secure enough rooms for everyone, though we were split between two motels. He told Mom, "I wanted to keep everyone together so I wouldn't lose anyone, but I couldn't make that happen." So, half the crew followed Dad, and the other half followed Rico.

Rico was born in the USA to immigrant parents, but his early years were challenging because his parents hadn't taught him English when he was small. He eventually picked up the language in school and became one of the few translators in his community. Rico and my dad had been friends for a very long time. As a teenager, Rico spent his summers picking fruit during harvest season in Central California while my dad worked as a mechanic. Later on, they both ended up working for the same farmer that my grandfather worked for, bringing them back together after high school. When Dad's friend from L.A. told him about a job opportunity at Western Geophysical, Dad signed on and immediately wanted Rico to join him.

Jobs in the oilfield working for a big company like Western Geophysical paid significantly better than farm work in Central California. Poverty rates were high in those small communities, so when the chance to work in the oilfields came along, many men jumped at it, eager to provide a better life for their families. Dad knew he could trust Rico with anything, and he valued their friendship deeply, so when the opportunity arose for him, he called Rico immediately.

Rico had a sharp sense of humor that always had everyone laughing. Most of his jokes revolved around his culture, and while Mom didn't always appreciate them, the guys on the crew found them hilarious. Dad also knew that Rico had plenty of friends who would jump at the chance to work in the oilfields and make what they called "the good money." Working on the farms didn't offer much in the way of extra comforts, but a job in the oilfields could change all that. That good money could send your kids to college and a better life.

Rico was not as tall as my dad, but he had the same work ethic. Work was what was going to pull them out of poverty, so both of them worked very hard and very long hours to make sure that their families would never need to struggle. Rico had a beautiful wife named Alma. Alma did not speak much English, but she always cooked and handed out food. She was a great cook and always had a little something sweet for all of us kids. Rico and Alma had three kids, who were about the same age as me, my sister, and my brother. Rico and Dad would travel together for a couple of years, and both families would become close. Rico's oldest daughter, Sonia, and I would become close friends, that is, until yet another move separated the families, and I would never see or hear from Sonia again.

Dad finished talking to the crew, and then he took half the crew with him to one motel while Rico took the other half with him to the other motel. We were only a short drive away from our motel. When we pulled into the motel parking lot, I was almost certain this place would not have air conditioning. The motel looked like it was a classic old highway stop, the kind you'd find along dusty roads in the 1970s. It sat quietly along an aging stretch of highway, a low-slung building with a faded sign that had seen better days. The parking lot was a mix of cracked asphalt and patches of dirt, and the whole place was coated in a layer of desert dust.

The motel had a tired look, with peeling paint and curtains that hung limply in the windows. It was the kind of place where you'd hope for air conditioning because, in the sweltering desert heat, the absence of a pool was a serious drawback. I remember spotting an old soda machine outside, the kind that hummed and clicked as it dispensed cold glass bottles, and I hoped Dad might treat us to a refreshing drink. After the long, hot drive from Bakersfield through the relentless desert, I could use a nice cold Coke!

Meanwhile, my brother and sister had slept the entire way, and now they were buzzing with energy, ready to raise a ruckus. Their noise and excitement were hardly what Mom needed after such a tiring journey and unexpected news, but they were unstoppable. The dusty old motel might not have had much to offer, but to them, it was a new playground where they could make as much noise as possible.

Mom was deep in thought, lost in the uncertainty of moving to Utah. I think she was more at ease with the idea of moving to Texas; like me, at least, she knew a little bit about the place. But Utah? None of us knew anything about Utah. Maybe she was also worried about what her brothers and sisters would think. They hadn't been happy about their baby sister moving in the first place, but Texas was something they could all wrap their heads around. It was familiar enough, but Utah was a different story altogether.

As she mulled over these thoughts, Mom seemed oblivious to Michael and Mia, who were running wild in the parking lot with some of the other kids from the crew. Dad, who was handing out motel keys to the men, finally lost his patience and yelled at me to get them under control. He was always yelling at me to keep an eye on those two brats. They weren't my kids, but somehow, I was the one responsible for them.

Reluctantly, I grabbed both of them by the backs of their shirts and started dragging them back toward Mom, who was still miles away in her own thoughts. It wasn't until Michael accidentally stepped on her open-toed shoes, causing her to yelp, "Ouch!" that she snapped out of her daze. The look of surprise on her face made it clear that she had been far away from the noisy, dusty parking lot in Blythe, lost in worries about a future that none of us could quite picture.

Dad finally finished handing out motel room keys to the crew, and they all eventually disappeared behind closed doors. We followed Dad to our room once he was happy that everyone was settled in for the night. "Please have AC! Please have AC!" I chanted silently in my head, my exhaustion making me almost desperate. Dad finally unlocked the door and swung it open. The instant the door cracked, a cool breeze rushed out to greet us, a refreshing contrast to the scorching desert air. It was like stepping into an oasis of relief. The room was cooler than the rest of the building, and that steady hum of the air conditioning was the sweetest sound I'd heard in ages. The room's air conditioning unit was an old window unit, clunky and noisy, but, at that moment, it felt like a miracle.

The motel room was definitely a relic from the '50s, with its distinctive decor reflecting years of wear and tear. The walls were lined with faded, flowery wallpaper that had seen better days, and the heavy, musty curtains did little to block out the harsh desert sun. The floor was covered in threadbare carpeting that had collected layers of dust over the years. The furniture was basic and utilitarian: a couple of full-size beds with old-fashioned bedspreads, a small wooden table with two chairs, and a bulky, outdated television perched on a dresser.

All I could think about was lying my head on a pillow instead of an open window sill. Before I could throw myself on the bed, Mom yelled, "Oh no, you don't! You kids need a bath first. Ughhh! I just wanted to go to sleep and sleep comfortably on a bed instead of in the backseat of a station wagon in the blistering sun. I didn't care about a bath. Mom told me to take my brother and sister into the bathroom and get them in the tub while she went back to the station wagon to get all of us clean clothes. I never understood why I had to take care of those two all the time. I hated taking care of those two brats. They were like little tornadoes in my life, causing much grief and making a mess wherever they went. A mess that I had to clean up. Maybe it was the long drive or the relentless heat, but I really hated those two brats right now.

Mom finally stepped out of her daze and went into mom mode. "Sonny," "You need to find a store close by and get some lunchmeat and cokes so we can feed the kids," she said in a mom-mode voice. "Michael and Mia haven't eaten anything except for chips since we left Bakersfield." All I could think about was how they ate all the chips and left none for the rest of us. Mom was always worried about those two. I remember thinking that she never worried whether I ate or not. I was just the babysitter to those two blond-haired, blue-eyed brats. For years, I blamed my red hair and freckles on the fact that they never paid attention to me, like they paid attention to those two.

I dragged those two into the bathroom to give them a bath like Mom said. The bathroom was just as dated as the main room. It had avocado-green tiles and a chipped porcelain sink that had seen better days. The bathtub had a stubbornly low showerhead, and the thin plastic shower curtain clung to the sides, giving a slightly claustrophobic feel. The tiny room was cramped, with barely enough space for the door to swing open fully without hitting the sink.

Mom came back into the room with clean clothes for everyone while I was still trying to get Michael to get in the tub. He wanted to play with the toilet and kept flushing it over and over. Then, he would turn around and start playing with the sink. I was tired of chasing this kid around the small bathroom and yelled, "Knock it off! Get in the tub!" His relentless energy was aggravating. Despite my attempts to calm them both, they continued to make lots of noise and splash lots of water. I could hear Mom yelling at me, asking me to stop yelling at my brother. She finally came into the bathroom with soap and shampoo from the car. She picked up my now naked little brother and put him in the tub. Then she looked at me and said, "Now wash their hair, but be careful not to get soap in their eyes." With half-lowered eyes and under my breath, I mumbled, "Really?"

Once my brother and sister finished their bath, it was my turn. It felt good to wash off the dust and sweat of the day. After my shower, Dad returned, and Mom started making sandwiches for everyone. The scent of fresh bread and ham filled the room, a smell that would soon become synonymous with our family travels. I hadn't realized how hungry I was until I scarfed down a whole ham sandwich faster than ever before, finding unexpected comfort in the familiar taste. Meanwhile, my brother and sister, still brimming with energy, were jumping up and down on the bed, their excitement at being in a new place spilling over.

I was trying to focus on my meal and the TV, but the chaos made it difficult. Mom's voice cut through the noise, "Stop jumping on the bed and eat your dinner!"

When Mom's yelling didn't work, Dad snapped his fingers, and just like that, they both froze and started eating. He had a way of commanding attention with a simple snap, a power that never ceased to amaze me.

They soon started arguing over what to watch on TV. I wanted to watch Happy Days, but they insisted on cartoons. Of course, they won, and we all ended up watching Looney Tunes together, their laughter filling the room. As we settled into the evening, Mom walked over to the open window, her gaze lingering on the view outside, perhaps finding her own moment of peace amidst the lively atmosphere.

"Sunsets in the desert are truly amazing!" Mom exclaimed, her eyes fixed on the view outside as she nibbled on her sandwich. We all got up and joined her at the window. She was right—the sight was mesmerizing. The fiery oranges and reds near the horizon gradually softened into pinks and purples, finally blending into the deep, velvety indigo of twilight.

As the day came to an end, everyone was full and content, ready to settle down for the night. We were all looking forward to sleeping in a nice, clean bed and gearing up for the next morning. Gazing at the rainbow of colors in the desert sky had softened my feelings about the trip so far. The warm shower, clean clothes, and a satisfying sandwich had helped, too. Dad even surprised us with a cold Coca-Cola, which was a real treat.

But while we were winding down, Dad was still a little tense. His thoughts were with the crew, worrying that someone might change their mind and leave in the middle of the night. The last thing he wanted was to be stuck in Blythe, California, waiting for a replacement to take over driving one of the big trucks. There was nothing he could do but wait—and maybe pray, though I knew that he wasn't doing the latter.

For now, though, we could all rest, letting the calm of the evening settle in, as the vibrant colors of the sunset slowly faded into night.

Chapter 2:
A New Path Ahead

That particular morning, Dad woke us up early, his voice tinged with urgency as he announced, clapping his hands together, "I need to check on the crew. Up and at 'em!" He appeared utterly exhausted, his face pale and drawn, with dark circles under his eyes betraying how little rest he had managed to get. Moving frantically around the cramped motel room, his movements were sharp and hurried as he tried to rouse everyone from sleep and push us toward the door. His voice was strained but determined as he turned to Mom, barely pausing as he grabbed a suitcase to throw in the station wagon. "Finish loading everything into the car," he instructed her, "I need to go talk to the crew. We're meeting Rico and the others at McDonald's, and I really need a cup of coffee." His words came out fast, filled with urgency as if every minute slipping by was pulling them further behind schedule.

Mom's pace quickened her calm exterior, beginning to crack under the mounting urgency. She hustled around the room, urging us kids to get up, her voice firmer than usual. "Let's go. Get up. Your father is in a hurry this morning." She was already moving with the precision of a seasoned packer, methodically loading the last of the bags into the car. Over the years, she would become a professional at this — packing everything up at a moment's notice, always ready to move, all while wrangling three young children.

She moved like someone who had done this countless times before, though the weight of the morning hung over her. Grabbing the last of the luggage, she managed to mumble something to Dad as he rushed out the door, "Don't worry, go check on the crew." Her words were more reassurance to herself than to him, as she shoved the final suitcase into place, every movement exuding efficiency and urgency.

Mom got everything out of the motel room, her movements brisk and efficient. After ensuring all of us kids were in the station wagon, she did one final walk-through of the room, her eyes scanning every corner. Just as she was stepping out, Dad appeared from across the parking lot. He eyed her with a hint of concern, "Did you double-check that we didn't leave anything behind?"

She shot him a glance, her eyes narrowed slightly, giving him that look that said he must think she didn't know what she was doing. "Of course, Sonny," she replied with a touch of exasperation.

"Good!" he said, satisfied, not paying any attention to Mom's exasperation. "Now, let's get over to McDonald's and grab some coffee. The crew that came with us is loading up their families and warming up the trucks. They'll meet us there."

With that, we pulled out of the motel parking lot, the station wagon rumbling down the road toward McDonald's, where the next phase of our journey would begin.

So, there we were, in Blythe, California, parked in the lot behind a McDonald's, barely awake while waiting for the rest of the crew to arrive. Dad had gone inside to grab breakfast for everyone, leaving Mom to open the rear of our station wagon, where my brother and I were sitting, taking in the cool desert morning.

There's something truly special about mornings in the desert. The world feels hushed, almost reverent, and the day's heat hasn't yet begun its relentless rise. There is a profound silence that envelops you as the sun starts to rise and the sky transitions from bright, sparkling stars dotting the deep blue horizon to pink and golden hues streaking across red rocky wind-blown outcrops. You can feel the cool air, and yet also feel the warmth seeping in ever so gently. As the light grows stronger, the details of the desert landscape become more defined. You notice the delicate patterns in the sand formed by the wind, the intricate textures of the cactus spines, and the small, hardy flowers that bloom in defiance of the harsh environment. A few birds begin to stir, their songs sharp and clear in the quiet morning. You might spot a jackrabbit or a lizard moving quickly to soak up the first warmth of the day. There is a sense of timelessness in the desert morning that is both invigorating and calming.

The parking lot was mostly empty, save for us and a couple of other vehicles that likely belonged to the workers already inside. I was especially hungry that morning, probably because we had eaten so late the night before. My brother was restless, fidgeting, and whining as his stomach grumbled. My sister had leaned over and gone back to sleep. Mom was sitting on the edge of the station wagon lid, holding my brother back, making sure he didn't fall off. "Sit down and be still," she scolded him, but he wasn't listening.

I could see Dad walking back toward us, balancing bags of food and his usual cup of coffee in his hands. Mom, of course, didn't drink coffee—back then, it was always sodas and sweet tea for her.

Dad sat next to Mom on the trunk of the station wagon, sipping his coffee while Mom handed Michael some fries from the bag of food Dad had brought. Michael was jumping up and down while Mom was trying to get him to settle down and eat. Dad snapped his fingers, and suddenly, Michael calmed down and started eating the food placed between his outstretched legs.

Dad, beaming with gratitude, turned to Mom and smiled, "Everyone in the crew that came with us is accounted for, and, to my relief, they've all agreed to make the trip with us to Utah." His voice was filled with genuine happiness, knowing that the day's plans were falling into place.

The crew was mostly a ragtag group of farmhands who had rarely ventured beyond the familiar fields and orchards of home. Although they were apprehensive about the journey, they seemed to be in relatively good spirits. Traveling to Texas was already a big adventure in their lives, and now, with the destination changing to Utah, a place that felt as distant and mysterious as another country, you could see the uncertainty on their faces, but also a tinge of curiosity. Dad told the crew to load up and meet us at the McDonald's right off the interstate. So, there we sat in the parking lot of McDonald's, waiting for the crew to arrive.

We were also waiting on Rico and the crew that went with him. It shouldn't be too long now, and Dad would finally know how to proceed. The uncertainty couldn't have been good for his nerves, and the waiting was boring for the rest of us. However, we were getting to eat at McDonald's, and that was always a treat.

McDonald's was one of the few chain restaurants you could count on back in those days. It seemed like every town had one, and for my dad, it was his favorite place to grab a quick bite. But McDonald's in 1974 was a totally different kind of place. The golden arches were iconic, standing tall and bright, and the building had that classic, mid-century modern design with sloping roofs and large, welcoming windows. Inside, the seating was simple—plastic booths with bright colors, often red or yellow, and the smell of fresh fries and burgers was always in the air.

There was no drive-thru back then, so you had to go inside to order. The menu was basic, with none of the endless options you see today. A burger, fries, and a small drink—that was all you really needed. Happy Meals didn't exist yet; the small meal was the "happy" meal in those days, and there was no big publicity surrounding toys or promotions.

McDonald's also had playgrounds, which were simple but exciting for us kids. They usually had a small slide or a set of swings, perfect for burning off some energy before getting back on the road. The place felt more like a local hangout than a corporate chain. It was familiar, comforting, and, in a way, it was a piece of home no matter where we traveled.

Dad sat beside Mom on the trunk lid of the station wagon, sipping his coffee and taking in the beauty of the morning desert. As the sun began to rise, the sky was painted with soft pastels, and the vast open spaces stretched out before us like an endless canvas. We all sat in silence, focused on eating our breakfast.

He pointed toward the horizon and said to Mom, "Can you believe this view?" His voice was gentle, as if the scene in front of him had momentarily lifted the weight of responsibility from his shoulders.

Mom smiled, responding, "Almost as great as last night's sunset."

Their quiet banter continued for a few more minutes, a rare moment of calm before the day's work began. Then suddenly, Dad stood up, stretching his back, and I could tell his mind was already on the road ahead. "I figured out our route last night, Millie," he said, looking down at Mom. "We'll go right through Las Vegas."

And with that, Mom stood up and proceeded to start cleaning up the wrappers from breakfast. I'm not certain, but I think she was ignoring him. My ears, however, immediately perked up.

Dad kept talking about the route and Las Vegas while shifting his gaze to the desert view. Mom remained silent, focused on my brother and sister. I couldn't help but wonder if Dad was subtly trying to convince her to stop in Vegas, perhaps now taking advantage of her preoccupation to get her to agree without fully realizing what she had agreed to. It wasn't entirely clear if he was speaking to her or just thinking aloud at this point, but his words spilled out without much pause.

"You know I've got an uncle in Vegas? He owns a small motel right on the strip. I wonder if he could accommodate the whole crew?" Dad's voice drifted into more of a mumble as he talked about how long it had been since he had seen his uncle. "It's been a few years since I've seen Uncle Jack. He's got to be about 70 years old by now. I wonder if Mom has his phone number. I should give him a call before we leave Blythe," Dad continued rambling.

I glanced at Mom, who remained entirely absorbed with my brother and sister, offering no response. It was hard to tell if Dad even noticed her silence. He seemed more caught up in his own thoughts now, as if he was mulling over the idea for the first time. Once Dad had an idea in his head, he usually didn't seek anyone's approval—he just went for it. And judging by the way he kept musing over his long-lost Uncle Jack, it seemed pretty clear that stopping in Vegas was becoming a serious consideration, with or without Mom's input. That was probably why she ignored his conversation.

The idea of visiting Las Vegas for the first time was beyond thrilling. I didn't really know what Vegas was like, except for what I had seen on TV—everyone always looked so happy, like they were living in a fantasy world filled with lights and excitement. My heart leaped at the thought of going. Woo hoo! I wanted to go to Vegas! I wanted to see those towering neon lights, the shimmering glamour, and maybe, just maybe, catch a glimpse of Dean Martin or Jerry Lewis. To me, Vegas was the epitome of fun and excitement.

I had only ever seen it through the TV screen, where it looked like the most dazzling place on Earth, and now the possibility of actually being there made my stomach flutter with excitement. Suddenly, breakfast didn't matter anymore. I could barely sit still as I imagined the flashing signs, the glittering casinos, and the energy of the bustling streets. My mind raced with visions of brightly dressed showgirls, sleek cars, and larger-than-life billboards. I was just a kid, but even I could sense that Las Vegas wasn't like anywhere else—a place that lived somewhere between a dream and reality.

As I sat there daydreaming about Vegas, my mind filled with images of neon lights, glitzy showrooms, and larger-than-life celebrities, the excitement bubbled up inside me. I could almost feel the electric atmosphere of the Strip, and the idea of actually being there was almost too much to contain. My heart raced with anticipation, my thoughts spinning faster than the slot machines I'd seen on TV. But then, just as I was lost in the thrill of what might be, a sudden shift snapped me back to reality.

A car pulled up beside us, and the mood changed instantly. A strange tension replaced the joy and excitement that had just filled the air. The parking lot was practically empty, with wide-open spaces stretching out in all directions. There was no reason for anyone to park so close to us, yet here they were. Why would someone choose to pull up right next to us when there were so many other spots available?

The carefree thoughts of Vegas I had been imagining moments ago now disappeared. My heart, which had been racing with excitement, now pounded for a different reason. Dad was suddenly on guard, and I could sense his concern. What had started as a day filled with anticipation and possibility suddenly felt uncertain as we sat there, wondering what this unexpected car was doing in the empty lot, parked so close it almost felt intentional.

Dad glanced over at the couple in the front seat, his brow furrowed. The car was a new hatchback, something we'd only seen on TV before. It was sleek and modern, painted a bright white with gleaming hubcaps that caught the morning sun. The whole back seat seemed packed full of belongings, so much so that you couldn't see into the car beyond the front seats. It was as if the car was bursting at the seams with whatever they were carrying.

What really caught my eye was the decal on the side of the car. It was official-looking, with bold letters spelling out "National Forest Service." The green and brown emblem of the Forest Service stood out against the white paint, a tall pine tree encircled by a shield. It looked like something you'd see on a ranger's vehicle deep in the woods, not in a McDonald's parking lot in the middle of the desert. The decal gave the car a certain authority, making me wonder where the couple had been or where they were headed.

Meanwhile, Mom was in the back of our station wagon, busy as ever, not noticing the car. The station wagon was now our mobile home on the road, and it had seen its fair share of chaos during yesterday's trip. Mom was organizing the belongings the kids had managed to scatter once again, her hands deftly folding clothes, tucking toys back into bags, and making sure everything had its place. She worked quickly but with a certain grace, laughing and playing with Michael and Mia as she did.

Michael had managed to lose a sock, which Mom found stuck in the crevice of the seat. "Look what I found, Michael!" she teased, waving the sock like a prize before slipping it back onto his foot. Mia was holding onto her favorite stuffed animal, which had lost its bow overnight. Mom tied it back on with a flourish, making Mia giggle with delight. Despite the mess, Mom had a way of turning the task into a game, keeping the little ones entertained while she restored some order to the chaotic little world.

While Mom was busy in the car with my little brother and sister, Dad and I were watching the couple get out of their car. The man was a skinny guy with glasses. He looked like some kind of scientist. The lady in the passenger seat had a sleeveless light blue shirt on. She looked like she belonged to that car, but he didn't.

The man stepped out and walked around the rear of the car, a broad smile on his face as he approached my dad. He was of average height, with sandy blond hair that was just beginning to thin on top, and his face was tanned and weathered, probably from spending a lot of time outdoors. He had a friendly, open demeanor, his eyes crinkling at the corners as he extended his hand. "Hi there! I'm David, and this is my wife, Nancy," he said warmly.

Nancy appeared from the passenger side, slightly flustered as she brushed off her shirt, which bore a few stray crumbs or perhaps a small stain from something spilled earlier. Her petite frame moved with an effortless grace that hinted at a life spent outdoors. Short brown hair curled softly around her sun-kissed face, her cheeks lightly flushed from the heat. She wore well-worn khaki shorts and sturdy hiking boots, her attire suggesting a readiness for adventure at a moment's notice. As she looked up, her eyes gleamed with warmth, and she gave a bright, welcoming smile, waving cheerfully. "Hi there!" she called out, her voice light and pleasant, perfectly matching her radiant, down-to-earth presence.

Though they both seemed nice enough, their sudden appearance and overly friendly demeanor struck me as a bit odd, especially since they had parked so close to us when the parking lot was practically empty. But I wasn't too concerned. My dad, standing a good two feet taller than David, cut an imposing figure, his broad shoulders and solid build making him look more than capable of handling any situation. I was pretty sure Dad could take on David and Nancy both with one hand tied behind his back if it ever came to that. Still, I couldn't shake the feeling that there was something a little strange about their approach, and I kept a watchful eye on them as they chatted with Dad.

Dad greeted him with a casual "Hi," while firmly reaching for David's handshake. But then, with a steady tone and a look that hinted at something deeper, Dad added, "I noticed your license plates say New Mexico. What brings you to California?"

I had a feeling Dad wasn't just making small talk. He was letting David know, in his own way, that he had noticed the details and could identify him if anything went sideways. It was Dad's way of sizing him up, using his presence and words as a subtle show of strength. He had always been the kind of man who could intimidate with just a look, and his size only added to that. Even though he seemed calm on the surface, I could tell Dad was being cautious, quietly making it clear that he was prepared for anything.

David's broad smile made it clear that he was either completely unaware or simply oblivious to Dad's cautious demeanor. As Dad subtly sized him up, David's grin only widened, completely unfazed.

"We just left Yosemite and are headed back to Capitan, New Mexico," David said cheerfully. "My wife works for the Forest Service, and she was sent to survey the damage from the fire in Yosemite." His tone was light, and he seemed completely immersed in his own story, completely missing the careful way Dad was assessing him.

Nancy nodded, her face growing serious as she added, "The recent wildfire in Yosemite National Park caused extensive damage to the forest wildlife. I was there documenting the results of that damage. It's heartbreaking to see such a beautiful place scarred, but it's important work."

Just then, David reached for the hatchback and popped it open. To everyone's surprise, two small black bear cubs poked their heads out into the cool morning air. Their fur was soft and glossy, their round eyes full of curiosity as they took in their surroundings. The little bears were the very image of wilderness, with their tiny noses twitching as they sniffed the unfamiliar scents in the air.

"Oh wow!" I exclaimed, excitement bubbling up inside me. Before anyone could react, I was off the trunk of the station wagon and racing toward the cubs. Dad reached out his long arm and caught me before I had a chance to get past him. He gave me a stern look that told me to stop running for their car and wait until I was invited over.

Mom, hearing my outburst, quickly came around to the back of the car. Her eyes widened in amazement as she spotted the bear cubs. "Well, would you look at that!" she murmured, more to herself than anyone else. The sight of the cubs was irresistible, drawing all of us in like a magnet.

The bears were so small, so full of life, and in that moment, the concerns of the morning seemed to melt away. The thoughts of Vegas and the strange arrival of David and Nancy were all overshadowed by the presence of these tiny symbols of nature's resilience. They were a reminder of the wild, untamed beauty of places like Yosemite, and for a brief moment, we were all connected by the simple joy of seeing these young creatures up close.

David smiled warmly as he spoke, "We noticed you had small children and were wondering if they'd like to interact with the cubs for a little while?"

I could hardly believe what I was hearing. Were they serious?

Dad's body language had been tense and guarded, his eyes sharp as he sized up David. But the moment he caught sight of the bear cubs in the back of David's car, everything shifted. His shoulders relaxed, and a smile tugged at the corners of his mouth. It was as if all the caution and intimidation tactics melted away in an instant.

"Are those bear cubs?" Dad asked, his voice softening as he leaned in for a closer look. Any hint of suspicion or wariness disappeared as the tiny cubs fidgeted in the back, their soft fur and playful movements disarming him completely. For the first time since David had approached, Dad seemed genuinely at ease, captivated by the unexpected sight of the bear cubs.

"Of course, my kids would love to play with the cubs," Dad exclaimed with a grin. But it wasn't just about us—I could tell Dad wanted to join in just as much. His eyes lit up with genuine interest, and the playful tone in his voice made it clear that he was just as eager as we were to interact with the little cubs. It seemed like letting us play was the perfect excuse for him to get in on the fun, too.

David explained, "Their mother was lost in the fire, and these little cubs have been full of energy ever since we left Yosemite. We're hoping that if they play with your children for a few minutes, it might help them settle down for the long ride back home to Capitan."

Nancy chimed in at that moment, "Bear cubs who lose their mother at such a young age often face a difficult journey. Without the mother's guidance and protection, they are vulnerable and in need of careful human intervention to survive. Interaction with people, particularly children, could help them develop trust and reduce stress, which is crucial for their well-being in the care of wildlife rescuers such as ourselves."

She continued, "Playing with children, who are closer to the cubs' own size, will provide a form of enrichment, allowing the cubs to engage in natural behaviors like play that are vital to their development."

"Wow! This lady sounds so smart!" I thought to myself as she spoke passionately about her work. At that moment, I knew exactly what I wanted to be when I grew up—a Forest Ranger. I wanted to be the one out there in the wilderness, protecting and saving all the forest animals. I wanted to help animals like these cubs, ensuring they had the best chance at survival. Helping them adjust to life without their mother, making sure they stayed active, healthy, and cared for during such a confusing and traumatic time—it felt like such a noble purpose. The idea of dedicating my life to preserving the forest and its inhabitants filled me with a sense of excitement and direction I had never felt before.

As I stood there, ready to meet the cubs, I felt a mix of excitement and a deeper understanding of the importance of this interaction. These little bears needed care and compassion, and for a few moments, we could provide them with a bit of comfort and companionship on their journey to a new life. At that moment, my memories of Brownie flooded in, and I wish I could have saved him like these people were saving the little cubs. My heart ached for these little cubs almost as much as it had ached for Brownie.

David glanced my way and motioned for me to join him at the back of the car. Dad put his arm down, letting me know it was ok to accept their offer to meet the cubs. David and Nancy carefully lifted the baby bear cubs out, gently placing them on the pavement. I lowered myself to the ground beside them, and almost instantly, the cubs began to explore me with playful curiosity. One of them nuzzled up to my leg, its tiny paws patting my knee as it tried to get a grip. The other one took turns nibbling on the laces of my tennis shoes, his tiny teeth tugging at the strings with a mix of determination and innocence. As I ran my fingers through their impossibly soft fur, I felt the warmth of their tiny bodies pressing against me, their playful energy contagious. Their little growls of contentment mingled with the occasional giggle that escaped my lips as they clumsily climbed over each other, eager for attention. It was a moment of pure, unfiltered joy, surrounded by these tiny, curious creatures, their innocence shining through with every playful bite and nuzzle.

Just then, my little brother Michael came sprinting over, his laughter echoing in the cool morning air. The moment the bear cubs spotted him, they seemed to recognize a kindred spirit, someone just as young and brimming with energy as they were. Their tiny eyes lit up with excitement, and before we knew it, they were chasing him around in playful circles. Michael darted this way and that, his feet barely touching the ground as the cubs tried to keep up, their little paws skittering on the pavement.

The cubs were relentless in their pursuit, but Michael didn't seem to mind; he was loving every second of it. Their soft growls mixed with his giggles, creating a symphony of pure, unfiltered joy. Meanwhile, my sister Mia, who came to see what all the excitement was about, stood a few steps back, peeking out from behind Mom's legs. Her wide eyes watched the scene unfold with a mix of curiosity and caution, but no amount of coaxing or gentle words could convince her to leave the safety of Mom's side. Mia's blonde wisps of hair fluttered in the breeze, catching the sunlight as she peered out from behind Mom's leg. The sight of Michael and the cubs playing so freely was tempting, but Mia remained rooted in place, her grip on Mom's leg tight, her face half-hidden yet entirely focused on the playful chaos before her.

As I sat there, gently stroking the cubs' soft fur, they continued to explore, circling around my brother with playful curiosity. Their energy was infectious, but it was clear they were always on the lookout for something more exciting. Nancy, sensing the perfect opportunity, reached into a cooler in the car and pulled out a baggie full of cut-up apples. The moment the cubs caught a whiff of the fruit, their attention snapped to her, eyes wide and eager. They were on her in an instant, tiny paws tapping against her leg as they reached up, noses twitching in anticipation.

One by one, the cubs grabbed slices of apple from her hand, chewing with enthusiastic, almost comical intensity. Their little jaws worked furiously, and as soon as they finished one slice, they looked up at Nancy expectantly, practically bouncing on their hind legs in a bid for more. Their excitement was palpable, their movements becoming a bit more frenzied as they nudged and nuzzled her leg, begging for another taste.

Nancy handed me a couple of apple slices, and I eagerly offered them to the cubs. They accepted them with a quick snatch, their small teeth crunching through the apple flesh with gusto. As I fed them, their eyes would flick back and forth between me and Nancy, making sure they weren't missing out on any treats.

Watching all this, Nancy turned to Dad and, with a nod toward Michael, said, "I don't think he's quite old enough to feed the cubs. We don't want any mishaps. Cubs can get a little aggressive during snack time." Her tone was light, but there was a note of caution in her voice, as the cubs, despite their size, could be a bit rough when food was involved. Michael watched with wide eyes, his laughter quieting down as he observed the cubs' more focused, determined behavior during their snack. The playfulness from moments before had given way to a singular focus on the apples, showing just how quickly their instincts could take over when food was on the line.

Mom walked around me, and Dad picked up Michael after Nancy's comment. Mom didn't want to take any chances.

However, I continued happily helping Nancy feed the last few remaining slices of apples to the cubs while Mia ran back to the car, her fear taking over.

Just then, the loud rumble of trucks shattered the peaceful silence of the cool desert morning. The crew from our motel pulled into the parking lot, their arrival announced by the noise of engines and the excited chatter of children tumbling out of cars. Dad looked up and said, "Well, here's our crew."

The once serene scene was now filled with the sound of slamming car doors, hurried footsteps, and the eager voices of crew members and their families. They quickly noticed the bear cubs and, with curiosity sparking in their eyes, began to move toward us, eager to get a closer look. Children pointed and tugged at their parents' sleeves while the adults exchanged excited murmurs.

Nancy and David exchanged a glance, sensing the growing chaos.

The playful calm from moments earlier was rapidly dissipating, replaced by the bustling energy of so many people and children. Nancy, with a hint of concern in her voice, said, "That might be too much interaction for the cubs."

Without hesitation, they began to carefully gather the cubs, guiding them back toward the hatchback. The cubs, who had been so playful and carefree, now seemed a bit overwhelmed by the sudden change in their surroundings, their little heads swiveling to take in all the new sights and sounds.

As they loaded the cubs back into the car, Nancy and David turned to us with warm smiles despite the abrupt end to the morning's peaceful encounter. "Thank you for your help," Nancy said sincerely.

David, with a wave, added, "If you're ever in Capitan, New Mexico, look us up."

With that, they closed the hatchback, and the car slowly pulled away, leaving behind the echo of the cubs' playful morning amidst the growing hustle and bustle of the day.

You could see the disappointment wash over the other children's faces as the car with the bear cubs pulled away. The playful excitement that had filled the air just moments before was quickly replaced with groans and murmurs from both children and parents alike. They chatted among themselves, voices tinged with frustration, wondering aloud why their kids hadn't gotten the chance to pet the cubs. Some children tugged at their parents' sleeves, their eyes still fixed on the car as it disappeared from view.

Sensing the growing dismay, Dad stepped in, his voice warm and reassuring. "I'm really sorry about that," he said, genuinely apologetic. Then, with a quick change of tone, he added, "But hey, who's hungry? Breakfast is on me."

The mood shifted almost instantly. The disappointment began to fade, replaced by the prospect of a hearty meal. The children's faces lit up, and parents exchanged nods, grateful for the distraction. The chatter softened, the tension easing as thoughts turned to what might be on the menu.

With Dad's offer, the chaotic moment dissolved into something more manageable. The earlier excitement over the cubs was now replaced with the anticipation of breakfast. The group began to make their way toward the McDonald's entrance, their spirits lifted, and the earlier disappointment was almost forgotten.

Just then, the familiar rumble of engines filled the air as the crew that had been with Rico began pulling into the McDonald's parking lot, one truck at a time. Each truck rolled in smoothly, their tires crunching over the gravel as they lined up in a neat, orderly row. The first truck stopped, and then, like a practiced routine, the next truck followed suit, pulling in right beside it. One by one, the rest of the trucks filed in, forming a solid line across the lot.

As soon as the trucks were parked, the families' cars followed closely behind, easing into the open spaces nearby. It was as if they had all coordinated their movements, each vehicle pulling in methodically, adding to the growing caravan in the otherwise quiet parking lot. The crew had officially arrived, and with them, an air of anticipation seemed to settle over the scene.

Dad's face lit up with relief and joy as he saw that everyone had made it safely. He waved them over, his voice booming with enthusiasm. "I'm so glad to see you all! Breakfast is on me!"

The next few minutes were a whirlwind of excitement as we all made our way into the McDonald's. The place quickly filled with the buzz of chatter—kids and parents talking all at once, their voices full of energy. As we settled into our booths and tables, the conversation inevitably shifted to the bear cubs. My mom and I couldn't help but excitedly recount the experience, describing how soft their fur was and how playful they had been.

The other kids listened wide-eyed, especially those who had arrived with Rico. Their faces lit up with awe as they realized we had actually petted bear cubs. Some of them groaned in frustration for not getting to McDonald's sooner.

The ones who had missed out kept asking us questions, their words tumbling over one another in a rush of curiosity and excitement.

"Wait, wait... so, did you actually touch them?" one of the kids stammered, wide-eyed.

"How soft were they?" another asked, almost breathless, struggling to get the words out fast enough. "Were they, like... scared?"

"And... did they make any sounds?" someone else chimed in, their voice filled with a mix of awe and envy.

You could feel the energy buzzing around the table. Everyone was talking at once, trying to piece together what they had missed. The air was thick with excitement and frustration as each kid wished they had been there in time.

Dad stood at the counter, trying to juggle the orders from some of the crew, and it was clear this wasn't his usual territory. The scene was a bit chaotic, with everyone talking at once, trying to decide what they wanted. It wasn't something he was used to, and you could see him struggling to keep track of who wanted what. Rico stepped in to translate for those whose English was too difficult for Dad to understand. Rico tried his best to translate for everyone, but it quickly turned into a bit of a comedy. With so many people talking at once, he struggled to keep up with all the orders, fumbling through the requests and occasionally getting things mixed up. At one point, Dad looked at him, eyebrows raised, when Rico confidently relayed an order for three cans of peaches. Despite the confusion, they managed to get through it.

Meanwhile, my brother, sister, and I ended up with a second breakfast, which was both great and unusual for us. We weren't used to getting two meals in one morning, but Dad didn't seem to mind. Maybe he was just overwhelmed by the sheer size of the crew and the flurry of activity around him. Who knows? He was probably too busy to even notice. For once, he seemed to let things slide, focused more on getting everyone fed than sticking to the usual routine.

Plates of pancakes, eggs, and sausage quickly disappeared as everyone dug in, the sounds of laughter and chatter filling the room. It would seem that everyone was in high spirits. Food seemed to have that effect on people. Prior to eating, everyone was grumpy, but after eating, everyone seemed happy.

It was at that moment, watching the chaos around me, that I realized just how similar people were to animals when it came to food. The way everyone rushed into the McDonald's, eager to place their orders, reminded me of those hungry bear cubs the moment they caught the scent of apples. The cubs had been restless, pawing at the ground, noses twitching with anticipation, just as the crew members had crowded the counter, eyes wide with hunger. It was as if the smell of food triggered something primal in both people and animals alike—an instinctual response that drove them forward, focused on one thing: satisfying that hunger. The parallels between the bear cubs' eager scramble for food and the crowd of people lining up for their breakfast felt almost uncanny, and I couldn't help but smile at the thought.

Dad looked around the bustling restaurant, watching all the families talking and the children playing, with a broad smile on his face. He was clearly grateful that every single one of the drivers had decided to make the journey to Utah. It wasn't just about the job anymore; it was about the camaraderie and the sense of community that had formed among all of us.

Slowly, everyone made their way back to the rear parking lot where the trucks and cars were parked. Little by little, the stragglers from the restaurant gathered, their conversations filled with curiosity and anticipation as they waited for Dad to discuss the route to Duchesne, Utah.

As the men circled around the trunk of the station wagon, Dad began outlining the travel plan with his worn-out map laid out on the trunk lid. I had stuck my head in between some of the men so I could hear what was taking place. Mom pulled the back of my shirt, dragging me into the back seat of the car and away from the men. I could still see and hear, so I wasn't sure what the point was. Dad's voice was steady and authoritative, yet there was an undercurrent of excitement that hadn't been there before. The drivers, with their practical questions—how long it would take to get there, how many stops they'd need to make—listened intently. These were all valid concerns, but Dad was holding back the most thrilling news of all.

Finally, with a spark in his eye, Dad dropped the bombshell. "If we can make it to Las Vegas in one day," he said, trying to keep his voice casual, "we'll spend the night there." He had made the decision somewhere last night while lying in bed, thinking about the crew.

There was a brief pause as the men processed what Dad had just said. Las Vegas was a name some of them knew well, a place of legend with glittering lights and endless excitement. Yet, for most of them, it felt so far removed from their everyday lives that it seemed almost unreal. And still, some had never heard of Las Vegas. They exchanged glances, some with curiosity, others with uncertainty, as if they weren't sure what to make of the idea.

One of the drivers leaned forward, asking in Spanish, "¿Vamos a parar en Las Vegas entonces?" The others nodded in agreement, their questions lingering in the air. Rico listened closely and then looked over at Dad, who stood there curiously waiting for a translation.

Rico, always the reliable translator, turned to Dad with a slight smile. "They want to know if we're really stopping in Vegas," he said. He paused, then added, "They're wondering what the plan is. They've heard about Vegas, but they're not sure what to expect."

Dad nodded, sensing the flicker of interest in their eyes. "Yeah," he said, encouraged by their reaction. "I've got an uncle there. We might be able to stay at his motel."

Rico translated again, his voice smooth and steady, and the men seemed to relax a bit more, some exchanging excited words in Spanish. Still, Dad could see that a few were apprehensive—Las Vegas was overwhelming in its own way, a place that could feel larger than life. But for now, the idea was alive in the air, with a sense of anticipation starting to build.

"I can call Murphy and let him know we're staying in Vegas," Dad continued, his voice steady. "He can arrange the motel rooms we'll need. I just need everyone to agree."

One of the older drivers, Juan, leaned forward and asked in Spanish, "¿Pero, vamos a poder pagar eso? Las Vegas no es barata." (But are we going to be able to afford that? Vegas isn't cheap.)

Another younger driver, Luis, chimed in with a nervous smile, "¿Y qué hacemos allí? No conozco a nadie en Las Vegas." (And what do we do there? I don't know anyone in Las Vegas.) Apparently, Luis had never heard of Las Vegas, which struck me as odd. I looked at him with a furrowed brow, wondering what planet he had been on.

Rico, ever patient and calm, listened closely to their concerns. He reassured them with a confident nod, saying in Spanish, "No se preocupen. El tío del jefe tiene un motel en la Strip. Vamos a ver si podemos quedarnos allí. No será como gastar en un hotel caro." (Don't worry. The boss's uncle owns a motel on the Strip, and we'll see if we can stay there.)

The men seemed to relax a bit, but their eyes still flickered with questions, unsure of what the reality of Vegas would be like. Luis, ever curious, asked, "¿Y qué hay que hacer en Las Vegas?" (And what is there to do in Vegas?)

Rico chuckled softly and turned to Dad, translating the gist of their questions. "Juan's asking if we can afford to stay in Vegas, and Luis is wondering what we're going to do there."

They spent the next few minutes telling Luis about Vegas and letting Juan know that the company would pay for the motels as usual. I couldn't help but feel a twinge of sadness for Luis. He was moving to an entirely unfamiliar place—Duchesne, Utah—without really knowing what to expect. Now, he was heading to another city, one he had never even heard of: Las Vegas. It was one thing to move to a new location, but to do so without speaking the language fluently only added to the uncertainty. If I were in his shoes, I would've been terrified. Yet, Luis didn't seem nervous or scared in the slightest. Instead, he seemed quietly curious, his eyes filled with wonder about the unknown that lay ahead.

I wish I could be more like Luis. He approached this situation with such calm curiosity, never letting fear take hold. While I would've been anxious, maybe even overwhelmed, he seemed to embrace the unknown with quiet confidence. It was inspiring, really—his ability to just go with the flow, no matter how unfamiliar the situation.

As more men began peppering Rico with questions, Dad was trying his best to keep up with the translations. Rico was firing off explanations left and right, but the conversations were quickly getting out of hand. Finally, Dad threw his hands up and said, "Tell them we're not blowing our money on the tables. We'll check out the sights, grab some food, and maybe relax a bit. If anyone wants to gamble, they can do that on their own." Rico relayed the message, and then everyone nodded in agreement.

They started chatting among themselves in rapid Spanish, voices bouncing between excitement and cautious optimism.

"¿Tú crees que vamos a ver a alguien famoso?" one of the drivers joked, laughter rippling through the group. (Do you think we'll see anyone famous?)

Another chimed in, "Ojalá tengamos buena suerte. Tal vez hasta ganemos algo." (Hopefully, we will get some good luck, and maybe we'll even win something.)

Dad, still watching their exchange, caught bits and pieces of the conversation and smiled. He could tell the mood was lighting, and their apprehension was slowly giving way to curiosity. Vegas, with all its mystery and allure, was starting to feel like a real possibility.

As the conversation continued, the men called out to their wives, who were lingering by their cars, hanging back and chatting among themselves. Hector, with a grin on his face, waved over at his wife, signaling that they were planning to head to Vegas. She raised an eyebrow but nodded in acknowledgment, giving him a knowing look.

Turning back to the group, Hector nudged Luis with a smirk. "¿Ya le pediste permiso a tu esposa, Luis?" (Did you already ask your wife for permission, Luis?) The other men chuckled, catching on to the joke.

Luis flushed slightly but laughed along. "Claro que sí," he said with a mock-serious tone. "No quiero problemas cuando lleguemos." (Of course, I don't want any trouble when we get there.)

The men broke into laughter, giving Luis a few light slaps on the back. "Siempre tiene que pedir permiso antes de hacer algo," one of them teased. (He always has to ask for permission before doing anything.)

Meanwhile, the wives continued to chat by their cars, smiling knowingly at the playful ribbing their husbands were exchanging. Dad, overhearing bits of the conversation, chuckled to himself as Rico quietly translated the jokes, filling him in on the banter. "Well, at least Luis knows how to keep things smooth at home," Dad said, grinning. Rico translated, and the men roared with laughter again, the earlier tension melting away as the group settled into a lighter, more relaxed mood. The excitement for the next leg of the trip and even the playful anticipation of Vegas now hung in the air.

While the Spanish-speaking men were teasing Luis, some of the others who spoke English had their own conversations with their wives, who were hanging back by the cars.

One of the drivers, Tom, glanced over at his wife, Mary, who had been standing with the other women, clearly amused by the playful chaos of the group. "Hey, Mary," Tom called out, walking toward her with a grin. "Looks like we might be making a stop in Vegas after all. What do you think?"

Mary raised her eyebrows while shifting her young daughter from one hip to the next. "Vegas? Are you serious?" she asked with a half-smile, clearly excited by the prospect of seeing Vegas.

Tom shrugged with a sheepish grin. "How often do we get the chance to see Vegas?"

Mary laughed softly, shaking her head. "You're just hoping to catch a show, aren't you?"

"Maybe," Tom said with a wink. "Could be fun, don't you think?"

Mary smiled, giving him a playful shove. "Alright, but no blowing all our money on the slots."

Another driver, Bill, leaned against his car, talking to his wife, Linda. "You okay with this Vegas stop?" he asked, trying to gauge her reaction.

Linda looked up at him with a grin. "I'm fine with it. Just make sure you're not planning on sneaking off to any of those casinos. I heard people who have spent their whole life savings at those places."

Bill laughed. "You know I'm terrible at gambling. Besides, I'm more interested in seeing what this city of lights is all about. Should be an adventure."

Linda nodded, seeming to relax a bit. "As long as it's just sightseeing, I'm on board."

The light-hearted exchanges continued between the men and their wives, their voices mixing with the playful Spanish teasing from the other group. The atmosphere shifted to one of growing excitement and curiosity as the possibility of stopping in Vegas became more real for everyone.

There was a collective sigh of relief mixed with excitement. The decision was made—Vegas was officially on the itinerary. The men grinned at one another, and the mood lightened even further as the group prepared to load back into their cars and trucks. The adventure was now set in stone, and the anticipation of bright lights and the unknown filled the air as we all got ready to hit the road once more, this time with a definite stop in Las Vegas ahead of us.

Dad's face lit up like I had never seen before. He looked like a kid on Christmas morning, eyes gleaming with the realization of a dream he had harbored for as long as I could remember. Vegas had always been a distant fantasy, something just out of reach for him. But now, it was within his grasp, and the idea of it—bright lights and the big city —was exhilarating.

As a family, we'd often gather around the television to watch the side-splitting antics of Dean Martin and Jerry Lewis. Their chemistry was magnetic—Dean, the smooth crooner with a devil-may-care charm, and Jerry, the zany, energetic comedian who could send us into fits of laughter with just a look. Dad would always chuckle along with us, his eyes gleaming with nostalgia as he told stories about their famous shows in Las Vegas. He'd talk about the allure of Vegas in those days—the glitz, the glamour, the marquee lights that lit up the Strip, and the big stars who graced the stage. Dean and Jerry were a couple of the biggest stars in Vegas in those days, their names shining like beacons in the desert night. Dad would lean back in his chair, a wistful smile playing on his lips, and say, "One day, I'd love to go to Vegas and see them live—just imagine the excitement of being in the audience, the laughter echoing through the room, and seeing those big stars up close." You could hear the passion in his voice, the way Vegas represented a dream of larger-than-life moments, a place where stars like Dean and Jerry made magic happen under the dazzling lights.

We were headed to Vegas, and the excitement was electric. For that moment, Dad and the crew weren't just farm boys—they were adventurers on the brink of stepping into a world they had only heard about in stories. Dad couldn't contain his enthusiasm; his eyes sparkled with anticipation, and he spoke with a newfound energy. The idea of Vegas, with its bright lights, endless entertainment, and the chance to see the stars he admired, had him practically buzzing. Some of the crew members shared that same thrill—they might have spent their days working the fields, but tonight, they were ready for something bigger. They were about to walk into a place where their everyday lives would be left behind, if only for a night, as they embraced the mystery and magic of a world that seemed larger than life.

With everyone finally in agreement about the plan, Dad announced with a huge smile, "Alright then. Let me make a few calls while everyone uses the bathroom and gets ready to leave." There was a sense of urgency in his voice as he headed toward the payphone on the far side of the parking lot. His pockets jingled with quarters as he walked, his mind already racing with the logistics of the journey ahead.

The parking lot was a flurry of activity, with kids running around, parents sorting their belongings, and people filing in and out of the restrooms. The crew was getting restless, double-checking bags and making sure everything was packed just right for the trip. The chaos of preparing for the journey hung in the air, making the anticipation palpable.

Dad reached the payphone, juggling a handful of quarters as he fumbled to get everything organized. He dropped a couple of coins, muttering under his breath as he bent down to retrieve them. Once he got the phone connected, he started giving instructions to Murphy, explaining the plan, and then called his mom to get Uncle Jack's number. After a bit of back-and-forth, he finally dialed Uncle Jack in Vegas, hoping that he could accommodate such a large crew.

Meanwhile, we all waited with a strange mix of excitement and nervous energy, unsure of what the next few hours would bring but ready for the adventure.

Chapter 3:
Viva Las Vegas

Dad exited the phone booth and began walking back toward the crew, his face a mix of relief and worry. He had just spoken with Uncle Jack, who confirmed that he could supply the rooms they needed for the night. However, there was a catch—there wasn't enough space for all the trucks and cars. Uncle Jack suggested an empty lot on the edge of town as a good spot to park the equipment and personal vehicles, but the downside was that the trucks and cars would be out of sight, leaving them vulnerable to break-ins.

As Dad walked back to the station wagon, his mind kept drifting back to what Murphy had said earlier about the trucks costing a fortune. He wasn't about to let anything happen to those trucks. The weight of responsibility hung heavy on his shoulders, but he pushed it aside for the moment and forced a smile as he motioned for Rico to meet him at the back of the car.

Once Rico approached, Dad's expression turned serious again. He said firmly but quietly, "It's a go for the rooms, but we have to leave the trucks in a parking lot outside of town. There isn't enough room to park everything at the motel. I'm not happy about that. Those trucks are worth too much to take any chances. Plus, I'm not sure people will want to leave their cars and personal stuff in a vacant lot away from view. I think we should see if anyone would be willing to stay with the trucks and cars, which means they will not get a night to spend in Vegas."

Rico raised an eyebrow but waited as Dad continued, "I have someone in mind for the job, but I want your opinion first. Do you think anyone from the crew would be willing to stay behind and keep an eye on the trucks and cars?" Dad looked intently at Rico, trusting his judgment but clearly not ready to leave this decision to chance. He needed someone reliable, and he knew Rico might have the insight he needed.

Rico had a pretty good idea who would be willing to stay behind—Juan. Juan wasn't one to splurge, not on himself anyway. He sent nearly all of his earnings back to his family in Mexico, making sure they had what they needed. He had a wife and two young kids waiting for him there, and every dollar he saved meant a better life for them. Spending money on a night out wasn't his style. Especially a night out in Vegas. Rico was confident Juan wouldn't mind staying behind to watch over the trucks.

But still, Rico wanted to hear Dad's thoughts. He leaned in a little closer and said quietly, "I have someone in mind, but who are you thinking?"

Dad paused for a moment before responding, but then, at the same time, they both silently said, "Juan. " They grinned at each other, knowing Juan's frugal ways and strong sense of duty to his family made him the perfect fit for the job. It was a moment of lightness in the middle of all the uncertainty, and they both knew they could count on Juan to look after the trucks like they were his own.

Dad turned to Rico and said, "Talk it over with Juan while I hit the bathroom. I've had way too much coffee." He shook his head with a grin before heading off, leaving Rico to handle the conversation.

Rico didn't waste a second. He sprinted over to Juan, who was standing quietly near his assigned truck, lost in thought. Juan was a middle-aged Hispanic man who dearly loved his family back home in Nuevo Leon, Mexico. His family had once thrived in the ranching community back in Mexico, but everything changed when the government seized their land, leaving them with nothing. With no other options, Juan had come to the U.S. to find work, desperate to support his wife and kids while also holding onto the hope that he could somehow help his father reclaim their ranch.

Juan's belief in this dream was steadfast, even though Rico wasn't as optimistic. He knew how strict the new government regulations were and doubted that Juan could ever get the ranch back. But Juan believed that a recent law passed by the new president offered a glimmer of hope, and that was all he needed to keep pushing forward. Rico admired Juan's unwavering determination, even though he thought it was futile. He had often encouraged Juan to bring his family across the border to be with him, to start fresh in the U.S., but Juan had too much pride. His family's legacy meant everything to him, and he wasn't ready to abandon it. No matter how difficult things got, Juan's pride and his sense of duty to his family always came first. This sense of duty would eventually be so strong that Juan would leave the crew and go back to Nuevo Leon, but not until much later, and another move to another state.

Rico approached Juan with a familiar grin, starting off with, "Juan, mi amigo." Juan looked up immediately, already sensing that something was up. Rico rarely called him "friend" unless there was more to it than just small talk.

"We need someone to stay with the trucks once we get to Vegas," Rico began in Spanish. "The man who owns the hotel doesn't have room for all the trucks and some of the cars. But he told us about an empty lot on the outskirts of town where we can park everything. Sonny isn't comfortable leaving the trucks, the family cars, and everyone's belongings there by themselves. So, we are looking for someone to stay in the vacant lot and watch over everything until the morning."

Juan listened closely, his face still and unreadable. As soon as Rico finished, Juan's response was quick and direct and in English, "What's it pay?"

Rico hesitated, mentally kicking himself for not anticipating that question. He knew Juan was here to make money, not just do favors. "I'm not sure," Rico admitted, scratching the back of his head. "I didn't think to ask, but I'll talk to Jefe, and I'm sure we can work something out."

Juan nodded slightly, his expression still serious. "You talk to the boss, then we'll talk," he said firmly.

Rico nodded back, feeling a bit relieved that Juan hadn't dismissed the idea outright. "Come on, let's head over to the station wagon and wait for the boss," he said. Together, they walked across the lot, the desert wind kicking up a bit of dust as they made their way toward the station wagon to wait for dad.

By the time Rico and Juan made it to the station wagon, Dad was just stepping out of the bathroom, wiping his hands on his jeans. Rico wasted no time, blurting out, "Juan wants to know what it pays?"

Juan stood there in his old, well-worn work boots, the leather cracked and scuffed from years of use in the fields and on the ranch. His shirt was tattered, the faded fabric streaked with dust and dirt from the desert air. It clung loosely to his frame, already damp with sweat as the sun began to rise higher in the sky, warming everything around them. His jeans, too, had seen better days, frayed at the edges and covered in the same layer of fine dust that seemed to coat everything out here.

Dad grinned, amused. He knew he should have anticipated that question, especially from Juan. "Well," Dad began, pausing for a moment as he calculated. He needed to be fair but also keep some cash on hand for Vegas. He glanced at Juan, sizing him up, before finally saying, "A hundred bucks for the night."

Juan, not missing a beat, nodded and replied in his broken English, "Throw in dinner, and it's a deal."

Dad chuckled, shaking his head in approval. "Deal," he said, clapping Juan on the shoulder. It was settled. "You drive a hard bargain, Mr. Echeverria."

Rico let out a subtle sigh of relief. He wanted to see Vegas and felt his excitement rise as the final hurdle had been overcome. Dad, too, looked relieved, a weight lifting off his mind as the final detail fell into place. As Juan returned to his truck, Dad and Rico smiled at each other, knowing they would get to see Vegas.

The sun was steadily climbing in the sky, and with it, the temperature was rising. It was already getting hot, and the heat was making everyone restless.

Families were starting to shift impatiently, the kids fidgeting in the backseats of cars. The women were fanning themselves with anything they could find. The dry desert air wasn't offering any relief, and it was clear that the sooner they got on the road, the better.

Dad hollered, "Let's load up and get this show on the road! Next stop, Vegas!"

Dad wiped his brow and turned to Rico. "We're taking Highway 95 all the way to Vegas," he said, his voice firm but with a sense of urgency. "So, let's get a move on." He glanced back at the crew and their families. "It should take about four hours to get there," he added, giving Rico a knowing look. "That's only if we don't run into any issues with the trucks—or the people—on this hot drive."

The trucks were loaded with gear, and the desert sun was starting to warm up fast. It was going to be a long, hot haul.

Each truck pulled out of the gravel parking lot, the crunch of tires on loose stone echoing in the dry desert air. One by one, they fell in line behind Dad's station wagon, forming a convoy as they made their way onto Highway 95, heading north toward Vegas. The sun was relentless, casting a harsh glare over the barren landscape. The heat seemed to shimmer off the asphalt, making the air almost unbearable. It was still morning and not yet noon, and already the heat was unbearable.

Dad had a plan to stop in Needles, California, for fuel and to let everyone stretch their legs, but that stop felt a long way off as we pressed on through the desert. The car's windows were all down, and the hot wind rushing in offered little relief. The breeze itself felt like it had been baking under the sun, and instead of cooling us down, it seemed to carry the heat deeper into the car.

My little brother and sister had dozed off in the back seat. Their bellies were full from breakfast. Their faces flushed red from the warmth, and tiny beads of sweat collected on their brows. I leaned against the door, staring out the window at the desolate stretch of road ahead. There was nothing in sight for miles in any direction—just endless cactus, scrub brush, and the occasional dirt devil off in the distance. The vast emptiness stretched on as far as the eye could see, making the desert feel even more oppressive.

As the minutes and miles passed, the heat quickly increased. It felt like a journey through an unforgiving furnace. The hot wind carried with it a fine grit of sand that stung our skin as it blew in through the rolled-down windows. It clung to us like a suffocating blanket.

I clutched my McDonald's cup; the ice had long melted, leaving only a warm, diluted soda swirling around. It wasn't refreshing, but it was still wet, and that was enough to keep me sipping. The sun beat down relentlessly, baking the asphalt beneath us until it shimmered in the distance, creating mirages of water that never came closer. The convoy moved steadily, but an unspoken tension was hanging in the air. It was a lonely road—no other cars in sight, just us and the endless stretch of desert.

The trucks rumbled ahead, engines groaning in the heat, and I think everyone silently prayed they would hold up. The thought of breaking down out here, in the middle of nowhere, was unsettling. We all hoped the trucks and cars could endure this oppressive heat as we pushed forward toward the oasis of Needles, our next stop on the journey.

Some of the families that had been trailing behind in the convoy grew impatient. The big trucks were only managing 45 mph at full speed, and the heat was unbearable. One by one, a few of the cars began to pull out from behind us, engines revving as they overtook the trucks and sped off down the road, eager to reach Needles faster. Dad was okay with that; he watched them go without a second thought. His priority was the trucks—they were the real lifeblood of this journey. Those massive rigs carried the goods that made the money, and if some of the families wanted to push past the 55-mph speed limit, that was their choice, not the company's concern.

Dad understood the oppressive heat all too well. He was feeling it, too. The air was thick and stifling, turning the inside of the car into a sweltering oven. Sand blew across the highway in ghostly waves, and the sun beat down with relentless intensity, bleaching the landscape and sucking the moisture from the air. Every breath felt like it was drawn from hell.

Mom wasn't faring much better. Her face was flushed red, sweat beading on her brow and dampening her shirt as she shifted uncomfortably in her seat. She glanced over at Dad, her patience running thin, and asked, "Can't we just meet the trucks in Needles too?" She wanted to speed up and get to Needles sooner, like those other families were doing. There was a note of desperation in her voice, her discomfort written plainly on her face. She wiped at her forehead and leaned back, catching sight of Michael and Mia. They were both sweating, too, their small faces flushed and sticky with the heat. Mom did not like the heat. At all.

Dad gave a sympathetic nod but remained resolute. He spoke firmly, "The trucks are my responsibility." And apparently, nothing was going to pull him away from them. The rest of the families could forge ahead, seeking refuge from the sun as fast as they could, but Dad, like the drivers behind us, was tethered to those big rigs. They were fragile beasts in this heat, and he knew all too well that keeping them moving was the difference between a successful trip and a costly delay.

As the cars sped past us on that blistering highway, a knot of tension seemed to settle in the air, heavier than the heat itself. This wasn't just about getting to Needles; it was about the choices Dad made—and would continue to make. That day wouldn't be the last time Dad picked those big trucks over his family. It would happen again and again, each time stretching the fabric of his marriage to Mom a little thinner.

Mom leaned back in her seat, her eyes narrowing against the sunlight, but there was more than just exhaustion in her gaze—a quiet frustration brewing beneath the surface. She was tired, and the heat added to her frustration. Over time, she would grow tired of moving, tired of being dragged from town to town, and tired of the job that seemed to consume Dad. With each new city came another change of schools for Michael, Mia, and me. Michael and Mia would struggle in class, which only deepened with each move. Later, we would learn that they both had a learning disability. But that wouldn't become common knowledge until they were both older and after many, many different schools. Mom had pleaded with Dad time and time again, telling him how the constant uprooting was affecting them, but Dad never seemed to hear her.

His loyalty was to those trucks—the big, lumbering beasts that paid the bills but demanded everything in return. Mom would soon learn that the job always came first.

She would watch it happen slowly, watching her marriage crack at the seams as Dad's job took precedence over our lives. Later, she would say she saw it coming but hoped to outlast the inevitable. That was one thing about Mom: she always had hope.

As we continued toward Needles, the road beneath us shifted from a smooth stretch of highway into a jagged, patchwork mess. It was as if the relentless desert sun had baked the asphalt until it cracked and crumbled, leaving nothing but rough patches and broken fragments. The car bounced and jolted over the uneven surface, and that harsh rocking was enough to rouse Michael and Mia from their sweaty slumber in the backseat.

Mia woke up first, her soft whimpers quickly turning into sobs as the heat bore down on her. "I'm thirsty!" she cried, tears streaking down her flushed cheeks. Michael started whining, too, though it was clear he wasn't sure why.

Mom, always the peacemaker, reached for her cup—now just a watery remnant of what had once been ice-cold soda—and handed it back to them. "Take a sip," she urged, her voice tense but soft, desperate to soothe them. But the moment the cup landed in their hands, chaos broke loose. Michael grabbed one side, Mia the other, both pulling and yanking at it like a lifeline. In seconds, it tipped over, spilling what little liquid remained across the seats.

Dad's scowl appeared instantly, his frustration boiling over. He snapped at Mom, his voice sharp and cutting. "I told you not to give them anything in the car!" His anger was hot, like the air that surrounded us, ready to ignite. All of us children suddenly got quiet for fear of Dad's anger.

Mom whipped her head around, her face flushed with more than just heat. "They're children, Sonny!" she shot back, her voice trembling with a mix of anger and exhaustion. "They're hot, they're thirsty, what do you expect?"

Dad clenched his jaw, his knuckles white as he gripped the steering wheel. He didn't respond; he just shot her a cold glare before turning his eyes back to the road. His gaze flickered to the rearview mirror, checking on the trucks behind us, the big rigs that were always more important than the rest of us. His silence only deepened the tension in the car, like a storm brewing just below the surface.

Mom sighed, reaching into the front seat for a rag to clean up the mess, trying her best to calm the chaos. Mia was still whimpering, her small voice grating against the silence that Dad had forced upon us. Michael sat there pouting, kicking the seat in front of him. I wanted them to shut up before Dad got furious, plus their incessant whining always got on my nerves. Tension and the heat continued to rise until I couldn't take it anymore—those two brats had pushed me too far. Without thinking, I lashed out, hitting them both in an attempt to get them to sit still and shut up.

That's when Dad's hand shot back, quick and angry, catching me off guard. He hit me hard enough to make my head snap back, and the sting of it settled deep in my chest. Silence fell again, heavier than ever, the oppressive heat filling the space between us, suffocating any chance of peace. Dad's eyes never left the road, focused ahead on the distant horizon, as if the trucks behind us were the only thing that mattered. Mom's hands trembled as she wiped up the spilled drink, her eyes downcast, defeated.

We were all trapped in that car—trapped in a cycle that felt unbreakable, like the desert heat that stretched endlessly around us, offering no escape.

That's the funny thing about heat—it strips people down to their rawest selves, exposing every hidden edge and sharp corner. It doesn't discriminate; it brings out the worst in everyone, adults and children alike. And for people who had never truly experienced heat like this, it was almost like stepping into a new realm of discomfort, where patience shriveled under the weight of the sun and tempers flared like wildfires.

We had never experienced anything like this heat before. We were used to cool breezes and shaded afternoons, not this relentless sun that burned through the windows and made the car feel like an oven.

In this kind of heat, everyone became a little more selfish, a little more desperate. Michael and Mia didn't care about the rules of the road; they just wanted something cool to drink, something to take away the constant prickling discomfort that had settled over their skin like a second layer. Dad didn't care about their thirst or their whining, not when the trucks were the priority, the only thing keeping his focus steady. And I—I just wanted them all to stop. The heat made it impossible to care about anything but my own discomfort.

Everyone sat in silence, each with their own thoughts. Michael and Mia eventually dozed off again, and I lay my head on the open window seal, pondering what life would have been like if only we had stayed in L.A. I was thankful that Brownie wasn't with us. He would have been miserable in the heat. I sure missed him, though. He was always happy. I dreamed of Brownie as I slowly drifted to sleep. We were running down the old dirt road headed to Deer Creek. The soft dirt was swirling in our footprints as we sped toward the tiny pond.

We never slowed down when we reached the pond. We both just jumped in and started splashing. Brownie would dog-paddle to the small beach and shake the water off his coat. Then he would jump back in and dog paddle back to the beach. The water was cool and refreshing, washing away the day's warmth. Oh, how I loved to swim in Deer Creek. Just me and Brownie and our own little hideaway.

Just then, I could feel the car slowing down. My dream would fade away, but not before I noticed I wasn't as hot as before. Maybe dreaming of Brownie and Deer Creek cooled me off in a way that reality couldn't. I slowly lifted my head off the windowsill to notice that we were pulling into a gas station. We must have made it to Needles. Did I sleep for two hours?

Mom told Dad, "Can you pull up closer to the bathrooms? Dad looked at her and said, "Sure." He added. "I'm going to go find a payphone and call Murphy. He needs to know that we made it to Needles with no problems." Mom mumbled something in agreement and then woke up Michael and Mia. "I'm going to the bathroom first!" I called out, knowing full well what would happen once Michael and Mia were up. As young kids, they always seemed to take forever in the bathroom—fiddling with everything, getting distracted, and taking their sweet time. If I didn't go before them, I'd be stuck waiting and holding. It would become its own miserable ordeal. Best to get ahead of the inevitable delay.

Dad had walked over to the dirt parking lot where all the trucks were pulling in. He was doing his usual check with the drivers, making sure the trucks were okay and not experiencing any problems. He suggested that everyone fill up now so we wouldn't waste time looking for a gas station tonight when we get into Vegas. Keeping track of all the trucks, all the drivers, and their families would consume lots of Dad's time. He seemed to like being in charge and seemed to have a knack for it as well.

Once I managed to secure the bathroom key, I couldn't help but notice it was attached to this giant block of wood. I wondered, who would ever steal a key attached to something so ridiculous? And why would anyone even want to steal a bathroom key in the first place? I didn't realize just how badly I needed to go until I sat down, finally getting a moment of relief. But that peace didn't last long—before I knew it, there was frantic banging on the door. It was Mom, her voice sharp. "Hurry up! Michael and Mia can't hold it! I am not dealing with any accidents on this trip!" Couldn't I have just one minute? But no, with my little brother and sister, even bathroom breaks were a race against time.

I rushed as best as I could in the old, dusty bathroom. The cracked tiles were stained with years of grime, and the single flickering light overhead made everything feel even more dingy. The floor was gritty under my shoes, and the musty smell made me wrinkle my nose. Mom was pounding on the door again. I would have to hurry or face her wrath.

When I finally opened it, her face was a mix of anger and frustration. I glanced down and saw why—Michael stood there with wet pants, the telltale sign he hadn't made it in time. The dark streaks ran all the way down his legs. And now, somehow, it was my fault? Totally unfair.

"Go dig out some clean clothes for him," Mom snapped.

I groaned, "But I wanted to get a Coke!"

That set her off. "No more sodas until we get to Vegas!" she screamed, her patience worn thin. It felt like I was getting punished for something that wasn't even my fault. All I wanted was a break from the heat and a cold drink, but now I had to dig through the suitcase for Michael's clothes. Ugg. He was such a baby.

I begrudgingly opened the back of the station wagon and started looking for the suitcase with his clothes in it. I had no idea where his clothes were or what to get him. In the meantime, I could see the other kids running around in the green field behind the gas station, playing tag and drinking their Cokes.

As I watched the kids through the station wagon window, Mom had come up behind me. "I asked you to get your brother a change of clothes!" she barked. "I don't know which suitcase his things are in!" I yelled back. Just then, Dad walked up. "What's going on? Why is the station wagon open?" He asked firmly. Mom's response was, "Michael had a little accident."

Dad's response, "Jesus, Millie. Could you not get him in there quicker?" They continued their back-and-forth arguing while I dug in the station wagon's heat. "Found it!" I said. Mom grabbed the suitcase and found clean clothes for Michael, then proceeded back to the bathroom, where Michael and Mia apparently made a mess by the way Mom yelled.

I was headed over to the small grassy area where the other kids were laughing and running around when I heard Dad's voice behind me. "Where are you going? Get back over here and fix the back of the car. Put everything back the way it was."

I froze, disappointment washing over me. I had been looking forward to joining the others, imagining myself finally having a little fun. Instead, I turned around and trudged back to the car. The back was a mess—suitcases shifted around and bags half-opened.

As I started reorganizing, my heart sank even more as I watched the other kids play without a care in the world. It felt so unfair, like every time I got a chance to be a kid, I had to miss out. This was Michael's fault. If he hadn't peed himself, I could have been playing and having fun.

After I finished reorganizing the mess in the back of the car, I finally made my way over to the small grassy area where the other kids were playing. Mom had walked Michael and Mia over to join while Dad was busy talking with the drivers and watching the trucks refuel. It felt a little cooler out in the open, especially in the shade, and I was eager to relax and have some fun.

Angie, a girl about my age whose dad was one of the drivers, had a soccer ball she was kicking around. I asked if I could join, and soon enough, we were kicking the ball back and forth, laughing and trying not to let it get away from us. The play area wasn't very big, just a patch of grass near the trucks, but it was enough for us to keep the game going.

As we played, the ball kept edging closer to the trucks lined up at the pumps. Dad glanced over his shoulder; his brow furrowed. "Keep that ball away from the trucks, or I'm taking it away!" he called out, his voice sharp.

Angie's mom heard Dad and quickly chimed in, "You girls need to be careful. Don't kick it so hard, okay?"

We nodded, trying to tone it down, but it wasn't easy in such a tight space. For a few minutes, we kept playing, but the fun started to fade a little. Every time we kicked the ball, I couldn't help but glance over at Dad, worried he might make good on his threat to take the ball away.

Mom sat on an old, worn park bench, watching Michael and Mia as they played with the other younger kids. Her face, once flushed from the heat and frustration, had softened a bit. You could tell the mood had shifted from what it was in the car earlier. It was still hot out, but now that we were in a grassy area with some shade, it made all the difference. The gentle breeze seemed to cool the air, and for the first time in hours, things felt a little more relaxed.

Mom was talking to Angie's mom, their voices low but steady, while keeping an eye on Michael, who had a tendency to wander off if you didn't watch him closely. I couldn't help but wonder what they were talking about. It was rare to see Mom chatting with someone new like that. She didn't make friends easily—she was always more of a loner, preferring to keep to herself.

But today, sitting in the shade and watching the kids, something was different. Maybe it was the temporary break from the road, or perhaps she was just too tired to stay withdrawn. Either way, seeing her actually engage in conversation with someone, even casually, was a rare sight. I watched them for a moment, curious, before turning my attention back to playing, feeling that little bit of peace settle in the air.

The cooler air in the shade would soon be a memory as all the trucks finished refueling, and Dad hollered, "Time to get back on the road!" It was a lovely few minutes while it lasted.

Back in the car and back on the road, the heat felt more oppressive than ever. The sun was beating down through the windows as if it were determined to melt us. The air was thick, and no matter how much we tried to adjust the window or fan ourselves, the heat was relentless. Dad, trying to lift the mood, glanced over at Mom and said with forced excitement, "Just a couple more hours, and we should see Las Vegas!"

Mom's face was flushed again, the same tired look she'd had earlier creeping back in from the sweltering temperature. Despite it, she tried to keep the conversation lively, as if she were determined not to let the heat win. "Yes! I can't wait to see the big city with all those flashing lights!" she said, her voice light but strained. She was trying, at least.

She kept going, almost as if to distract herself from the discomfort. "I wonder if they'll do the MD Telethon in Las Vegas again this year?" Mom asked. She loved the Muscular Dystrophy Labor Day Telethon. Every year, she got excited about it, always talking about how she wished she could be one of the telephone operators, answering calls for hours. It was one of her dreams, though we all knew it was something that would probably never happen.

Still, it was nice to hear her talk about it, something to break up the stifling silence inside the car. But as the heat bore down on us, the conversation, like the air, felt thin. Mom's attempts at conversation were noble, but I could tell she was wilting under the weight of the heat. The thought of reaching Las Vegas, with its lights and excitement, felt like a distant promise. All we could do was keep driving, hoping the next couple of hours would pass quickly.

The road stretched out endlessly before us like it had no intention of ever ending. Each mile seemed to crawl by, the scenery blending into one monotonous blur of dust, cactus, and endless patches of sagebrush. The sun had been beating down on us for hours, the heat relentless and unforgiving, making every second feel longer than it was. There wasn't much to look at—just the same dry, barren landscape mile after mile. Even the occasional tumbleweed drifting across the road felt like a small event in the otherwise empty desert.

But then, something began to shift. As we inched closer to Las Vegas, the vast emptiness of the desert didn't seem to matter as much. A subtle but growing sense of excitement began to build in the car. The dull scenery started to give way, first to a few scattered homes on the outskirts of town, then to billboards promising big winnings at casinos with names that felt larger than life—The Sands, The Golden Nugget, Caesar's Palace. Bright, colorful advertisements stood out against the desert backdrop, teasing at the glamour and energy that awaited us just ahead.

Suddenly, the last few miles weren't just part of an endless drive anymore. They were leading us to something exciting, something different. The closer we got, the more I could feel the change in the air. The dull, suffocating heat that had weighed on us for hours seemed to lift, replaced by an electric anticipation. The boredom of the desert faded as my eyes took in the towering billboards, the promise of lights, noise, and life just around the bend.

I found myself forgetting about the heat, the discomfort of being packed into the car, and the hours of dull scenery behind us. All that mattered was that we were almost there, almost to the bright lights of Las Vegas. The sight of homes, billboards, and the distant glow of the city on the horizon made the heat feel like a distant memory, and all I could think about was the excitement waiting for us in the city ahead.

Then, all of a sudden, as we crested a small rise, we caught our first glimpse of Las Vegas, and it was unlike anything I had ever seen.

Towering casinos stretched toward the sky, seemingly hundreds of them, their massive structures lined with flashing lights that blinked and shimmered in every direction. It felt like we had entered another world, one where everything was larger than life. The city itself seemed to glow, even in the daylight, the neon signs flickering and pulsing with a life of their own.

The excitement in the car was palpable. We were so close now, just on the edge of it all. My heart raced as I stared out the window, my eyes darting from one casino to the next—Caesar's Palace, The Stardust, The Flamingo—each one more dazzling than the last. It was overwhelming in the best possible way. The sheer size of it all made my jaw drop, and for a moment, I couldn't even speak.

"Look at that!" Mom exclaimed, pointing out a massive billboard for an Elvis show. Oh, how she loved Elvis!

Dad grinned, his earlier frustration melting away as he said, "This is what I was talking about—Vegas, baby!"

The heat, the long drive, the dusty desert—it all faded away as the city came into full view. We were almost there, just minutes from stepping into a world of lights, sounds, and excitement that felt like something out of a dream. I could hardly wait.

Dad found the exit we were instructed to use, and there was a large empty lot for all the trucks and cars. We pulled into the graveled parking lot, and one by one, each truck lined up with the cars pulling in behind. There was a payphone on the sidewalk, and Dad jumped out of the car and exclaimed, "Let me call Murphy and my uncle and let them know we have arrived!" I had never seen my dad so excited! Mom too! Michael was standing up in his seat, jumping up and down. Normally, Dad would yell at him to sit down, but Dad didn't even notice. He was living in the moment of being in Las Vegas.

It was as if a wave of excitement swept through everyone. Car doors swung open, and families began spilling out, stretching their legs and breathing in the warm desert air, but this time, the heat didn't seem to matter. Everywhere you looked, people were grabbing suitcases, digging through the backs of their cars, and chattering with excitement. The long, exhausting drive felt like a distant memory now that we were in Las Vegas..

Parents called out to one another, coordinating who was riding with whom for the short trip into town, where the motel was waiting. "We'll follow you!" someone shouted, while another parent waved, calling out to their kids to stay close. The air buzzed with anticipation as everyone sorted themselves out. There was a joyful chaos in the air, the kind that made everything feel more alive.

Kids were bouncing on their toes, practically vibrating with energy. Some of them were jumping up and down, their eyes wide as they caught glimpses of the neon glow in the distance, imagining the bright lights and bustling streets they had heard so much about. "I want to ride with Angie!" I heard one kid yell while others darted between cars, laughing and pulling at their parents' sleeves.

Even the adults couldn't hide their excitement. The usual exhaustion from long hours on the road seemed to vanish, replaced with eager smiles and hurried conversations. Dad finished his phone call and stood near the trucks, talking with some of the other drivers, his voice lighter than it had been all day. "Alright, let's get packed up and head in," he said, his grin contagious as he clapped someone on the back.

For once, Mom wasn't barking orders or stressing about the details. Instead, she was caught up in the moment, too, smiling as she talked with another mother about the arrangements. "I can't believe we're finally here," she said, her face glowing as she glanced toward the lights in the distance. It was the rare kind of moment when everything felt right, like we were all sharing in the excitement of something big.

Soon enough, families were piling into the few available cars, the sound of doors slamming and luggage being tossed into trunks filling the air. The conversations were fast and overlapping, kids calling dibs

66

on seats and parents trying to corral their families, but it was all filled with an undercurrent of joy. The hum of engines starting up felt like a countdown, each car ready to take off toward the glowing city ahead.

I could hardly sit still, my own heart pounding with anticipation. This was it—we were about to experience Las Vegas. The excitement was electric, and as we all prepared to make our way into town, it felt like the adventure was just beginning.

We loaded into a few cars, everyone buzzing with anticipation as we prepared to head toward the heart of Las Vegas. Dad made sure Juan was settled with the trucks, promising to bring him something to eat before we headed to the Strip. Juan gave a nod, his usual stoic expression softening as he watched us go. I felt a twinge of sympathy for him, left behind to guard the trucks while the rest of us were about to experience the excitement of the city. But Dad assured him he'd bring back food, and that seemed to be enough.

As our small caravan of cars pulled away, the drive felt surreal. The desert landscape we had been surrounded by for hours was quickly replaced with the vibrant energy of the city. The lights, even from a distance, cast a glow over everything. The excitement in the car was palpable, every face hanging out the windows, trying to take in as much as we could.

We passed by a large, iconic sign that read "Welcome to Fabulous Las Vegas, Nevada" in bright, bold letters, standing proudly as a gateway to the city. It was massive and glowed in the evening light, instantly recognizable even to a first-time visitor. I remember thinking that this was the sign I had seen in postcards, and now here it was, right in front of us. Mom pointed it out, smiling widely as she said, "There it is! The famous sign. It looks just like it does on TV!" Her excitement was contagious, and even Dad grinned as we passed it, nodding in appreciation.

The bustling energy of the city streets now replaced the quiet, desolate drive through the desert. Neon lights from the casinos illuminated the entire Strip, flashing reds, blues, and greens, casting colorful reflections on the cars around us. The casinos seemed impossibly tall, towering over the streets with their enormous marquees advertising shows, jackpots, and celebrities. I couldn't take my eyes off them. The Stardust, The Sands, Caesar's Palace—they were all there, larger than life.

People swarmed the sidewalks, tourists with wide eyes and big smiles, locals dressed sharp, heading in and out of the casinos, their laughter and chatter spilling into the street. Even though we were still in the car, the energy outside felt infectious. The streets were filled with taxis and limousines, and you could hear horns honking and music playing from open windows. It was like nothing I had ever seen—everywhere you looked, there was something happening. The excitement was electric.

Dad, usually focused and serious, was caught up in it too, pointing out the casinos to us kids. "Look at that! The Golden Nugget. That's a famous one," he said, his voice filled with a mix of awe and pride. Mom leaned forward in her seat, her eyes wide as she took it all in. "I can't believe how many people are here," she murmured, more to herself than anyone else.

We passed by a huge, illuminated fountain in front of one of the hotels, water dancing in the lights as people gathered around to watch. I could barely keep up with all the things happening outside my window—the billboards, the flashing signs, the crowds of people—it was overwhelming, but in the best possible way.

As we finally approached my uncle's motel, tucked away on the Strip but still close enough to feel the pulse of the city, I felt like I was stepping into a new world. The lights, the noise, the pure energy of it all—it was everything I had imagined and more. The excitement wasn't just out there on the street; it was in the car with us too. We couldn't wait to get out and experience it for ourselves.

Dad led the way for our small convoy, and as we drove down the bustling Strip, the city lights quickly gave way to a quieter, almost forgotten corner of town. The small, single-story motel we arrived at looked like something straight out of the 1950s, with its faded neon sign and old-fashioned design. There were about ten rooms, each with a chipped and weathered door, and from the looks of it, none were occupied. The place had a certain charm, like it had seen better days, but still held onto a slice of the past.

As we rolled to a stop, a tall, balding man emerged from the motel's main office, wiping his hands on his jeans and squinting into the setting sun. That must be Uncle Jack. He had the same broad shoulders and determined expression as Dad, though his hair was considerably thinner, and his face was etched with the lines of time. Still, he looked vibrant and full of life, his smile wide and genuine as he spotted the convoy pulling in. There was no mistaking the excitement in his eyes—he was thrilled to see us.

Uncle Jack's grin stretched even further when he saw Dad in the lead car. He waved enthusiastically, motioning for Dad to pull up right near the office. The two of them exchanged a knowing look, and you could tell Uncle Jack had been waiting for this moment, probably for years. As Dad eased the car into the spot near the office, Uncle Jack was already moving closer, eager to greet his nephew.

The rest of the cars pulled into the vacant parking spots, the quiet hum of engines slowly dying down. The atmosphere was different now, calmer but still filled with a buzz of anticipation. Uncle Jack practically jogged over to our car. "Well, well, look who finally made it!" Uncle Jack boomed, his voice filled with joy.

Dad grinned, stepping out of the car and meeting his uncle with a firm handshake that quickly turned into a hug. "Good to see you, Jack," Dad said, his tone lighter than I'd heard all day.

Uncle Jack laughed, clapping Dad on the back. "You too, kid! It's been way too long. I wasn't sure you were ever gonna get out here!" He looked past Dad at the convoy of cars and gave a nod of approval. "Brought the whole crew, huh?"

"Yeah, had to make sure we all got here in one piece," Dad replied with a smirk.

Uncle Jack motioned toward the vacant rooms. "Well, you've got your pick of the place! No one's around, so settle in wherever you like. I've got some cold drinks in the office if you need 'em."

The rest of the families started climbing out of their cars, stretching and breathing in the cooler evening air. You could feel the collective sigh of relief as everyone settled into the peaceful atmosphere of the motel after the long drive. Uncle Jack's laughter echoed through the lot as he greeted each family, his energy contagious. The old motel, though small and worn, now felt like a welcoming haven.

For a moment, it was as if we had stepped back in time, away from the bright lights and chaos of the Strip. Uncle Jack's excitement to see Dad—and all of us—made the place come alive.

Uncle Jack greeted each of us kids with a big hug before letting Mom know which room would be ours. Mom ushered us into a room by the office to freshen up while Dad followed Uncle Jack back to the main office. I'm not sure how long Dad was gone—it felt like forever. We were all eager to head back down the Strip, but Mom reminded us to be patient and let Dad and Uncle Jack have some time to catch up.

While watching out the bay window of our room, waiting for Dad to emerge, I saw a few of the families head out and down the street. I was getting excited, as was my mom, who was yelling at my little brother to stop jumping on the bed.

Finally, I spotted Dad emerging from the main office with Uncle Jack. They shared a hug, and Dad gave him a pat on the back before heading our way. It was clear Dad wanted to spend more time catching up with his uncle, but the excitement of the Strip was calling him. He seemed torn between the two.

At last, Dad opened the door and asked, "Are you ready?"

Mom raised an eyebrow. "Aren't you going to freshen up?"

Dad grinned. "Hell no. I don't want to waste any more time. Vegas won't even notice."

And with that, we headed out into the bright lights and buzz of the Strip.

As we stepped out of the motel parking lot, the sun had nearly disappeared behind the horizon. The warm evening air wrapped around us. With each block we walked, the glow of neon lights grew brighter, and the sounds of the city swelled around us. The hum of slot machines, the chatter of excited crowds, and the distant music all blended into a chaotic symphony.

Before we even realized it, we were in the heart of the action. It was dazzling, overwhelming, and impossible to take in all at once. Lights flashed in every direction, their brilliance intensified by the darkness of night. The streets were packed with people, and Mom quickly scooped up Mia while Dad hoisted Michael onto his hip, both of them determined not to lose us in the sea of faces.

Every step forward felt like a new adventure. I spotted someone I swore was Elvis, but Mom shook her head and said it was just an impersonator. A woman dressed like Marilyn Monroe passed by, her white dress billowing slightly as she walked. Showgirls in glittering costumes with enormous feathered headdresses breezed past us, their vibrant plumes catching the light as they disappeared into the casino doors.

Every flash of neon, every sound, every face—it was all a sensory overload, yet I couldn't stop staring. Vegas was alive, and for the first time, I felt like I was right in the middle of its beating heart.

Dad turned to Mom with a spark of excitement in his eyes. "Let's find Caesars Palace—that's where I want to go first."

We walked for what felt like forever, our feet growing tired on the crowded sidewalks. Suddenly, Dad pointed across the street, his grin stretching from ear to ear. "There it is!" he exclaimed. His pace quickened, and we scurried after him, weaving through the crowd and crossing the street.

Caesars Palace was breathtaking. The towering building seemed to stretch endlessly into the night sky, its golden lights glowing against the darkness. At the grand entrance stood a massive stone lion, majestic and imposing, guarding the circular driveway where sleek cars glided in and out.

We carefully navigated through the steady stream of cars and reached the towering glass doors. Through them, I could see rows of slot machines spinning and blinking, their bright lights flashing like police sirens. The air buzzed with excitement—people laughed, machines dinged, and everything shimmered with a sense of possibility.

It felt like we were stepping into another world—a world of endless lights, flashing colors, and the promise of something extraordinary just around the corner.

As Dad stepped through the towering glass doors of Caesars Palace, a sharply dressed gentleman approached him with a polite but firm expression. "Are you staying at the Palace?" he asked, his eyes flickering toward my little brother.

Dad replied, "No," and started explaining our visit, but the man quickly cut him off. "No one under 21 is allowed in the casinos," he said flatly.

Dad's face fell, his excitement dimming in an instant. He tried reasoning with the man, his voice calm but edged with frustration, as he attempted to salvage the moment. But the man remained firm.

Finally, Dad asked, "Are there any casinos where kids are allowed?"

The gentleman offered a polite but unyielding smile. "Vegas wasn't built for kids," he replied simply.

With that, he gestured us back toward the door. Dad's shoulders slumped slightly as we turned around and stepped back into the warm

Vegas night, the dazzling lights behind us feeling a little less bright.

You could see the sadness in Dad's eyes. I was sure he'd take us back to the motel, but instead, he said, "Let's try another hotel and see what they say."

And so, we went from one hotel to the next—each one delivering the same disappointing answer: "No children allowed in the casinos."

At one point, Mom offered to take us back to the motel herself, but Dad shook his head. "No, let's keep trying," he insisted.

Hotel after hotel, rejection after rejection, until we finally reached The Golden Nugget. A kind gentleman at the entrance listened to Dad's story, then smiled and said, "You should try Circus Circus. They let kids in there."

Dad's face lit up, and without hesitation, he hugged the man and thanked him over and over again. Holding Michael a little tighter to keep him from squirming away, Dad asked for directions. The man pointed down the street and said, "You can't miss it—it looks like a circus tent."

As we made our way through the crowded sidewalks, Dad suddenly pointed ahead. "There it is!" he said excitedly. And the man was right—it did look like a giant circus tent, except it was a building.

As we got closer, we spotted a giant sign proudly declaring that Ringling Bros. was performing that night. The energy outside was electric. Street performers were scattered everywhere—men dressed as Uncle Sam towered above the crowd on stilts, and another man in a top hat stood nearby with a monkey on a leash.

I'd seen monkeys at the zoo before, but never one walking calmly on a leash like a tiny, exotic dog.

The lights, the sounds, the sheer spectacle—it was like stepping into a magical world where disappointment didn't stand a chance.

We walked past the excitement outside and stepped into an even more dazzling scene inside. Showgirls in glittering costumes glided through the crowd, serving drinks with bright smiles, while women with painted clown faces juggled pins back and forth, laughing as they performed.

Michael started crying, overwhelmed by the noise and chaos, while Mia clung tightly to Mom, her little arms wrapped around her neck. It was sensory overload—bright lights, loud sounds, and movement everywhere.

Dad spotted a gentleman near the entrance and asked, "Are kids allowed in here?"

The man nodded. "Yes, but they must stay with their parents at all times. No wandering around."

A huge smile emerged on Dad's face!

With that reassurance, Dad hurriedly led us further inside. He reached into his pocket, pulled out some coins, and approached a slot machine. His hand shook slightly as he nervously dropped the change into the slot.

We all huddled close, watching intently as Dad grabbed the handle and gave it a firm pull. The reels spun, the bright symbols blurring together.

"Come on, lucky seven!" Dad said, his voice half-joking, half-hopeful.

The first spin came up empty—nothing. But on the second spin, a loud clink-clink-clink echoed as coins started pouring into the tray below.

Dad grinned and turned to Mom. "You wanna try?" he asked, his face lit up with excitement.

For a brief moment, it felt like we were all part of the magic of Vegas—a family in the middle of the flashing lights and ringing bells, sharing a moment of joy amidst the chaos.

With a determined grin, Mom grabbed a handful of coins and started playing the slot machine next to Dad. I stood there watching them for a while, mesmerized by the flashing lights and ringing bells, until something caught my eye overhead—a man on a trapeze.

He swung back and forth, gaining momentum, preparing for a daring jump to the next trapeze bar. My heart raced as I waited for him to leap, but my view was blocked before I could see the final catch. The distant cheer of the crowd told me he must have made it.

As the night wore on, Mom and Dad stayed glued to their machines. Dad said he didn't want to "push his luck" by moving to another one. Hours seemed to slip by unnoticed as the repetitive clinking of coins and spinning reels filled the air.

Eventually, I gave in to my aching legs and sat down next to Dad's machine. Michael had fallen asleep, and Dad gently laid him down between two machines, out of everyone's way. Mia was nodding off, too, curled up in Mom's lap, her tiny head resting against Mom's shoulder.

My stomach started growling, and I quietly told Dad I was hungry. "Hold on," he said without looking away from his machine. So much time passed that I eventually forgot about being hungry.

I sat there, people-watching, as Mom and Dad stayed locked in their little world of blinking lights and clattering coins.

I saw all kinds of people come and go—some excited, some disappointed, others stubbornly focused on their machines. One older woman caught my attention. She was deep in conversation with a man I assumed was her husband. He was clearly ready to leave, tugging at her arm and throwing out suggestion after suggestion: "Let's go eat. Let's go see a show." But she just shook her head, her eyes never leaving the machine. "This is the one," she said firmly. "I can feel it."

The man sighed heavily, defeated, and leaned against the nearby machine. I couldn't help but feel bad for him.

At that moment, I wondered if my parents were going to stay there all night too. The bright lights of Circus Circus felt endless, and time seemed to stretch into something unmeasurable.

As I sat there, watching the endless stream of people and flashing lights, a deep, rumbling sound caught my attention. I froze—it sounded like an elephant. My heart raced as I jumped up, scanning the crowded room and weaving my gaze through the sea of slot machines and people.

And then I saw it—at the far end of the building, an enormous elephant being led toward the big tented area. My excitement bubbled over, and I instinctively started walking in that direction, eager for a closer look.

But just as I took my first few steps, a woman sitting next to Dad suddenly shot up from her machine. Her face was flushed with anger, and she started yelling and cursing at the slot machine. "It took all my money!" she screamed, her voice sharp and wild.

The scene was so intense that I immediately backed away, stepping closer to Dad and staying out of her path.

Soon, a couple of men in suits arrived and gently escorted her toward the exit. But she wasn't done—her voice carried through the casino as she shouted about her losses, her words sharp and desperate.

The commotion was enough to break Dad's focus. He turned to Mom and said, "Maybe it's time to go. It's almost 2 in the morning, and we've got a long drive ahead of us tomorrow."

Mom glanced at her machine and hesitated. "Just a few more minutes," she said.

But Dad shook his head firmly. "Nope. It's time for the crazies to come out."

Neither Mom nor Dad ever hit the jackpot that night, but it didn't seem to bother them. On the way out, they laughed and talked about their losses, joking about how the machines had "eaten" their money.

Despite the late hour and empty pockets, their spirits remained light, and the magic of that night stayed with us as we stepped back into the warm Vegas air.

Walking back to the motel felt like stepping into a completely different world. Despite the late hour, the streets were alive with energy. Showgirls in glittering costumes strutted past, and the neon lights seemed even brighter against the deep night sky.

Traffic crawled along, packed with colorful hot rods revving their engines as they cruised down the Strip. Their polished exteriors gleamed under the glow of the flashing signs. Dad grinned and said, "Jimmy would love this," as we paused to admire a line of cars roaring past.

At one point, we even spotted an old Model T. Dad couldn't help but point it out, smiling as he said, "My grandfather used to drive one of those."

Mom held Mia tightly, her little body still fast asleep, while Michael woke up and squirmed in Dad's arms, craning his neck to get a better view of the dazzling line of cars.

The walk back felt endless, my tired feet dragging with each step. But as I glanced around, I couldn't shake the feeling that once we reached the motel, all this excitement—the lights, the sounds, the magic—would fade away forever.

I slowed my steps, trying to take in every detail, every flash of color, every sound. But Mom's voice cut through the night: "Keep up!"

Eventually, we made it back to the motel. As I collapsed onto the bed, exhaustion washing over me, I felt a deep sense of happiness. This night was something special, something I'd never forget.

And with that final thought, I drifted into sleep, the bright lights of Vegas still flickering behind my closed eyes—until Mom's gentle voice woke me the next morning.

As we stood by the station wagon, waiting for Dad to emerge from the motel lobby with Uncle Jack, I felt a twinge of sadness. It felt like we had only scratched the surface of Las Vegas, barely glimpsing what the city had to offer.

When Dad and Uncle Jack walked toward the car, Jack spoke up with a wistful smile. "Well, that's too bad. You should've taken the kids inside to see the circus. They've got a woman who rides a lion, a monkey who rides a giraffe, and an incredible trapeze show. Maybe next time, Sonny." Dad replied, "Yup. Maybe next time."

Those words stayed with me because there never was a next time. That was the last time Dad ever saw Uncle Jack. A couple of years later, Dad got a phone call with the news that Uncle Jack had passed away from some kind of illness.

It would also be more than thirty years before I'd see Las Vegas again.

Chapter 4: Duchesne

We piled into the cars and headed back to where we'd left the trucks. It was still early morning, and the sun had yet to rise fully, though a faint glow stretched across the horizon. Michael and Mia were fast asleep in the back seat of the station wagon, their faces peaceful in the dim light.

I kept my eyes closed, but the soft murmur of voices outside the car reached me. The adults were talking about their night in Vegas— some voices were animated, excitedly recounting the dazzling lights and sounds, while others carried a hint of regret as they spoke about money lost.

One person mentioned trying to get tickets to see Elvis, only to find the show sold out. Little did I know then that there would be two times in my life when I'd have the chance to see Elvis—and I'd miss both of them.

Another woman chatted about eating at an all-you-can-eat buffet. I'd never heard of such a thing before, but the thought of endless food reminded me just how hungry I was. I hadn't eaten dinner the night before, and now my stomach was aching.

I slowly opened my eyes and noticed Mom sitting quietly in the front seat. I leaned forward, tapped her on the shoulder, and whispered, "Are we going to eat something? I'm starving."

She turned slightly and said, "I'm sure Dad will stop somewhere on the way out of town."

I hoped she was right because the hunger pangs were getting worse.

Peering out the window, I noticed a few adults wandering around, stretching their legs and chatting, but I didn't see any other kids. I figured most of them were still curled up asleep in the cars, just like Michael and Mia.

It wasn't long before we were back on the main road, heading north out of town. Dad had mentioned earlier that it would take most of the day to reach Duchesne—if we made it that far. He had mapped out our route that morning while talking with Rico.

"U.S. 91 should take us all the way to Utah," Dad said confidently. I overheard him tell Mom he hoped to reach Provo before dark, if at all possible.

As the miles stretched on, Mom and Dad continued talking. They reminisced about the slot machines, the old cars cruising the Strip, and the bright lights of Vegas. Both of them agreed they'd have to come back someday. Dad wanted to spend more time in the city, maybe catch a show, while Mom dreamed of exploring the interiors of the grand casinos she couldn't enter because us kids were with them.

As their voices became a soft hum in the background, I started drifting back to sleep. A thought flickered through my tired mind: Maybe they shouldn't have had kids if they didn't want to miss places like Vegas.

My dreams carried me away—to Grandma's house, where Brownie and I would race down to Deer Creek, splashing in its cool water. Those days felt so peaceful, so simple. Back then, I never felt like a burden. I was always off somewhere—running through the grapevines, exploring the cotton fields, or playing in the walnut orchard.

I was never hungry then, either. There was always something to eat—cherries plucked straight from the trees, grapes fresh off the vines, snacks that seemed endless and effortless.

But now, my stomach's persistent rumbling broke through my dream and jolted me awake. I leaned forward again and asked Mom, "Are we stopping to eat soon?"

She turned back, her voice gentle but tired. "I'm sure your dad will stop soon."

I sank back into my seat, hoping her words would come true as the long road stretched endlessly ahead.

Just then, Dad spotted the sign. He could always see it from miles away—the golden arches of McDonald's. He was a die-hard fan, and back in those days, there weren't many other fast-food options in the U.S., which suited Dad just fine.

He flipped on the blinker, signaling to the convoy behind us that he was pulling off the highway. We rolled into the McDonald's parking lot, and Dad hopped out to make sure everyone else followed. One by one, the big trucks pulled in, their engines rumbling, followed by the family cars, forming a familiar caravan.

"Let's grab a quick bite and get back on the road," Dad said as he stood by the car, surveying the scene.

While Mom worked on waking up Michael and Mia, I wandered toward the car where Angie was sitting. But Dad's voice cut through the early morning air: "Get back over here and help your mom with Michael and Mia!"

Are you kidding me? Babysitting—again. Once more, I wouldn't get to play, chat, or even stretch my legs properly.

I trudged back to the car, grabbed Michael's hand as he tried to dart away, and pulled him in the opposite direction while he squirmed. Mom picked up a groggy Mia and carried her inside.

We finally made it through the glass doors of McDonald's and found a booth. Dad was still outside talking to Rico, and soon Juan joined them. Mom sat Mia down next to her on the bench and called out to Dad, "Just get whatever!"

Dad waved her off, still deep in conversation, so Mom sighed, turned to me, and said, "Watch the kids while I order our food."

I slumped onto the table, resting my head on my folded arms. Hunger gnawed at my stomach, and Michael squirmed endlessly on the bench next to me. I spotted Angie across the restaurant and gave her a quick wave, hoping she'd come over. But she didn't.

If I didn't have to watch Michael and Mia all the time, maybe I'd actually get to make a friend. But it felt like that was never going to happen.

Mom eventually returned with trays of food and set them down in front of us. She carried a cup of coffee out to Dad, who said he'd eat in the car because he still needed to talk to the guys.

I didn't waste any time—I scarfed down my eggs and gulped my milk, my eyes watching the crew as they came and went. I could've eaten more, but that was all we had.

Mom had gotten Dad an Egg muffin—a brand-new menu item that everyone was raving about. Usually, Michael and Mia barely touched their food, leaving me to claim their leftovers. But not this time. They cleaned their plates completely.

It was clear—I wasn't the only one starving that morning. And honestly, it sucked because I would've gladly eaten whatever scraps they left behind.

Once everyone had finished eating and climbed back into their cars, Dad slid into the driver's seat and said, "Let's get as far north as possible."

With a full belly and the day already warming up, I leaned my head against the window and quickly drifted off to sleep.

I don't know how long I slept, but it must have been a while because Dad's voice eventually woke me. "Look! The sign says, 'You are now entering Utah!'"

None of us—and I mean none of us—had ever been to Utah before. The only thing I knew about the state came from Mom, and that was mostly about the Mormons. I didn't really know what that meant other than they were religious, like Mom.

Great. Just what I needed—more people like Mom and her religion.

Mom was the youngest of 13 kids, and every single one of her siblings belonged to a different church. It made no sense to me. How could there be so many religions, all claiming to believe in the same God? They couldn't all be right. Someone had to be wrong.

Back then, I thought all my aunts and uncles were a little nuts for following so many different faiths. Couldn't they see what seemed so obvious to me? They couldn't all have the one true answer. At least one of them, probably more, had to be wrong.

That realization planted a seed of doubt in me, a distrust of the whole system. And honestly, it's something I still wrestle with to this day.

Dad turned to Mom and said, "We've been on the road about five hours. We need to stop for gas and grab something to eat. That Egg McMuffin was good, but I could've eaten two of them."

It seemed Dad was just as hungry as the rest of us. Skipping dinner definitely changes your mood the next day—apparently, even for grown-ups.

I sat up in my seat and looked out the window. The view hadn't changed much—it still looked like the desert we'd been driving through for hours. Had we really been traveling for five hours? Off in the distance, I could see what might be mountains, but they were still too far away to be certain.

Dad pulled into a small gas station just past the Utah state line. I don't remember the name of the town, but it was tiny. With our convoy of trucks and cars, it felt like we had invaded the place.

I realized I needed to pee, but I knew I'd have to help with Michael and Mia first. "Come on, let's go to the bathroom before everyone gets out," I told them. They both perked up, and Mom said, "Good idea."

Mom got out too, but she couldn't keep up with us as we raced toward the bathroom. The door wasn't locked—yes! I helped Michael and Mia first, then quickly took my turn. I could hear Mom knocking on the door, and Michael was trying to open it, but luckily, he couldn't reach the knob.

I hurried up, let Mom in, and noticed a line had already formed outside. It seemed like everyone else had been holding it, probably afraid to ask to stop in case they got left behind.

I waited by the door for Mom, and when she finished, she grabbed Michael's and Mia's hands and walked them back to the car. I spotted Angie nearby and stopped to talk to her, but before I could say much, Mom hollered, "Come on!"

Back at the station wagon, we waited while Dad spoke with the men running the gas station. One of them, an older guy, had taken off his ball cap and was scratching his head as if he was struggling to answer a question Dad had asked.

Time dragged on as all the trucks and cars filled up with diesel. We waited in the station wagon, the sun now fully up and pouring its relentless heat onto the car. There was no breeze, and the stifling air made it feel like we were baking in an oven.

Mom fanned herself with a piece of paper while Mia, now sitting in the front seat with her, leaned against her shoulder. Michael, on the other hand, was restless. Mom gave him some crackers she had stashed in the car, but he wouldn't sit still. He squirmed, whined, and then—of course—dropped one of his crackers onto the floorboard.

He immediately started crying, his nose running as he wailed about the lost cracker. Mom, clearly fed up, yelled at me to pick it up. Why couldn't he pick it up himself?

Grumbling under my breath, I reached down, grabbed the cracker, and handed it back to him. Anything to stop the whining and avoid more yelling from Mom.

Through the windshield, I saw Dad standing in front of one of the vibrator trucks, talking to the drivers and pointing north. Maybe there's a place to eat up ahead, I thought. I hoped so, because I was hungry again, and Michael wasn't the only one feeling cranky.

Finally, Dad walked back to the car and leaned into Mom's window. "We're going to head into town, grab some things to make sandwiches, and then drive to a little rest area the gas station attendant told me about. That way, we won't have to drive the trucks through this little town, and everyone can eat and stretch their legs."

Mom nodded in agreement and said, "Ok."

Dad climbed into the station wagon and drove into the small town while the rest of the crew waited patiently back at the gas station. This was definitely small-town America—nothing like L.A. or even Bakersfield.

Dad followed the old man's directions and found the town's one and only grocery store, sitting right across from the town square. Honestly, I don't think we could have gotten lost even if we tried— the town was that small.

Before stepping out, Dad turned to us and said, "Stay in the car while your mother and I go inside."

Great. Once again, I was stuck babysitting Michael and Mia.

Even with the windows rolled down, the heat inside the station wagon was stifling. Sweat clung to my skin, and the air felt thick. Meanwhile, Michael and Mia climbed over the seats, bouncing around like restless puppies.

From my spot in the car, I could see the grocery store's large bay windows. Handwritten signs taped to the glass advertised deals: "Eggs – 79¢ per dozen" and "Bread – 3 loaves for $1."

Two wooden benches sat on either side of the entrance. An elderly woman occupied one of them, clutching a brown paper bag of groceries in her lap. She looked like she was waiting for someone to pick her up.

The minutes dragged on, stretched out by the relentless heat and Michael's constant squirming. It felt like an eternity, though I'm sure it wasn't nearly as long as it seemed.

Finally, Mom and Dad emerged from the store, their arms weighed down with brown paper bags filled with groceries and six-packs of glass-bottled Coca-Cola.

Relief washed over me upon seeing them both. Left alone in an unfamiliar town with the responsibility of watching Michael and Mia, a heavy knot of anxiety tightened in my chest. My heart pounded, my breaths felt shallow, and the weight of being both a child and a caretaker pressed down on me.

With groceries in hand, we headed back to the gas station, where Dad instructed Rico to let everyone know to follow him. We got back on the highway and drove a short distance until we pulled into what looked like a small rest area—if you could even call it that. It was an open patch of land with a few weathered picnic tables and a single tree, or maybe it was just a large bush, offering a scrap of shade.

Dad parked the station wagon, and one by one, the big trucks and family cars followed, pulling in behind us. Everyone climbed out, stretching their stiff legs and breathing in the dry desert air. I was just relieved to be out of the station wagon—it felt like I had been baking in an oven back there—and I was starving.

Mom and Dad carried the groceries over to one of the picnic tables and started unloading the bags. They had bought supplies for sandwiches—bread, lunch meat, cheese, and condiments. The sodas weren't cold, but they were wet, and in that heat, even lukewarm soda felt like a treat.

Mom, along with one of the other mothers, got to work making sandwiches while a few of the men gathered under the sparse shade of the lone tree.

For a brief moment, I got to sit and chat with Angie and a couple of the other kids. It felt good to have a little bit of freedom, to share a moment without Michael and Mia hanging off me. I even managed to tell Angie how much I loved the beach compared to this dry, dusty desert.

But the break didn't last long. Dad stood up, clapped his hands together, and announced, "Alright, time to pack up. We've got to get back on the road!"

The moment was over just like that. At least I got to say hi to Angie and share a few words. It wasn't much, but it was something— a little breath of fresh air before the long road stretched out in front of us again.

Once everyone was loaded back into their cars and we were back on the road, Dad pointed ahead and said, "Look in the distance—I see mountains!"

Mom squinted toward the horizon and added, "Yeah, and I also see what looks like rain clouds."

"Oh, how wonderful it would be to get some rain," Mom had said exactly what I was thinking.

As we got closer to the mountains, the air began to cool, and slowly, raindrops started to splatter against the windshield. Before long, the rain came down hard enough that we had to roll up the windows. With them up, the air inside the station wagon felt thick and stuffy. But with them down, rain blew in on us, making everything damp. And if it wasn't wet, it felt humid.

Through the streaks of rain on the glass, I couldn't see much—just more stretches of desert landscape blurred by the downpour.

We drove for about three more hours through the sporadic rain and gusting wind before Dad said, "We should be coming up to Provo. We've been on the road all day—it's probably a good idea to stop there for the night."

Provo. What a strange name for a town, I thought. I couldn't help but wonder where the name came from.

"Mom, where did the name Provo come from?" I asked.

She shrugged. "I have no idea."

That got me thinking again. Where did the name Duchesne come from?

Once again, Mom replied, "I have no idea."

During those long stretches of road throughout my childhood, I would often wonder about the origins of the towns we passed through. So many names, and so few answers.

When I got older, I could simply ask Google to find out. But in the early 1970s, there was no Google—just curiosity and unanswered questions tucked away in the back of my mind.

Even now, as an adult, I still find myself Googling the history of town names whenever I pass through a new place. I'm sure that habit was born from those endless road trips, where questions piled up with no way to find answers.

It's funny how the small curiosities of childhood can follow you into adulthood, shaping habits and quirks you carry with you for a lifetime.

Dad was right—we were close to Provo. I had just spotted a road sign that read: "Provo, Utah. Elevation 4,549 ft."

I wasn't sure what elevation meant, but it was important enough to put on a sign.

The sun was beginning to set as we pulled into town. Dad found a rest area, and like clockwork, the big trucks and family cars followed, pulling in one after another.

Once again, Dad told us to "Stay in the car."

Seriously? All I wanted was to stretch my legs. It felt like we were living in this car.

Outside, the other drivers climbed down from their trucks and gathered in front of Dad's station wagon. I could hear their muffled voices as Dad unfolded his trusty map across the hood.

"We've got a couple more hours of driving ahead of us," Dad said, "but it's getting dark, and everyone's tired. It's probably best if we stay here for the night and head out fresh in the morning."

Some of the men didn't seem comfortable with the idea of sleeping at a rest area, but Dad reassured them. "It's better than spending money on another hotel room."

Rico chimed in, "It's only a few hours." Then he repeated in Spanish. Juan said something in Spanish, and everyone shook their heads like it was okay.

Rico translated: "Juan said that we could always lock the cars, and there was safety in numbers."

Dad had planned this trip down to the mile, but for some reason, we had only made it to Provo instead of Duchesne before nightfall. Dad wasn't usually wrong about these things. I heard him say while he rubbed the back of his neck, "It's the rain, the slower driving speed, plus the elevation."

Curious, I asked Mom what elevation meant.

"It means how far up a place is from the ocean," she said matter-of-factly.

What? That made no sense to me. What did this place have to do with the ocean? I stared out the window, trying to make sense of her explanation, but before I could ask more, Dad appeared at Mom's window.

"I'm going to send Rico into town to get supplies. I think it's best if we stay here for the night."

Mom's face fell. "What do you mean we're staying the night at a rest area?" Mom looked up, clearly flustered. Apparently, she hadn't heard Dad and Rico talking just moments ago. Her mind was focused on Michael and Mia and keeping them occupied.

But Dad didn't answer. He turned away, walked over to Rico, handed him some money, and gave him instructions to head into town. I watched as Rico drove away, hoping that he would return soon.

So, I guess it was official: we'd be spending the night at this little rest area. We'd eat dinner here, try to get some rest, and head out in the morning.

Mom was not happy, and from the looks on their faces, neither were many of the other women.

Some of the kids were allowed out of their cars to run around, laughing and stretching their legs. But not us.

"Can't I at least stretch my legs?" I asked Mom, hopefully.

"No," she snapped. "Wait for your father."

I slumped back into my seat, staring out at the fading daylight, wishing I could at least feel the gravel under my shoes. The night ahead felt long already.

When I saw Rico return with supplies to make sandwiches, I was relieved. I would always worry when someone left the safety of the crew. I'm not sure why.

We were finally allowed out of the cramped station wagon to eat. Thank God. I had felt stiff, hot, and utterly miserable sitting in that car for so long.

We ate our sandwiches and drank warm sodas under the night sky. But the real treat was stretching our legs, running around, and laughing with the other kids. The air was cooler now, and the night felt calm. It was a much-needed change of pace after such a long, hot day on the road.

Mom told us kids to sit on the gravel by the bench, promising to bring us sandwiches. I spotted Angie across the way and waved. After getting her mom's approval, she came over to join us. Her brother and sister tagged along, and soon, all of us kids were sitting together on the gravel, munching on sandwiches and sipping our warm sodas.

"I can't wait to get to Duchesne!" I told Angie with excitement.

"Me too!" she replied, her eyes lighting up. "I've got a bike, and we can go riding."

I sighed and said, "We had to leave our bikes in California."

She grinned and reassured me, "Don't worry, I'll share mine with you."

We chatted and laughed, our conversation flowing easily as the warm evening settled around us. Eventually, Angie's mom called out, "Come on, time to get some shut-eye." With a few quick goodbyes, Angie and her siblings disappeared into the night, leaving behind the happy buzz of our little gathering.

After they all left, I felt exhaustion creep in. My body was heavy and sleepy when Mom called us back to the station wagon. She had pulled out several bags from the back and arranged a makeshift bed for us kids.

I groaned internally. Sleeping next to those two again. They squirmed, kicked, and shifted all night long. And let's be honest— there was a good chance one of them would pee on me.

Mom climbed into the back seat, curling up with a blanket, while Dad sat outside. He wasn't ready to sleep yet. I could still hear his voice drifting through the night air as he sat at a nearby picnic table with the other drivers. They sipped warm sodas and smoked their Marlboros, their low voices blending with the soft hum of the traffic passing nearby.

Eventually, Mom was asleep, Michael and Mia were out cold, and the night grew still.

I lay there staring out the window, the faint glow of the distant trucks providing a little light. A small wave of fear crept over me— sleeping in a rest area didn't exactly feel safe. But then I reminded myself of what Juan had said: We're not alone.

We were surrounded by our convoy—big trucks, family cars, and a whole group of people who felt like our own traveling community. Maybe, just maybe, we'd be safe tonight.

With that thought, I let my heavy eyelids close and finally drifted off to sleep.

I woke to Michael nudging me in the shoulder with his elbow. Groggily, I opened my eyes and brushed him away. It took me a moment to gather my bearings. I was in the back of the station wagon. Mia was still asleep beside me, and Mom was curled up in the back seat. Outside, Dad was standing with a group of drivers, sipping coffee and talking quietly. I couldn't figure out where they had gotten the coffee. I thought they had gone to a store, but later Mom told me one of the women had brought along instant coffee and shared it with the group.

I gently shook Mom awake. She stretched, yawned, and sat up. The morning was still and quiet, with a faint mist in the air, though the warmth of the day was already settling in. I climbed over the seat and stepped out of the station wagon in search of a bathroom. To my dismay, there wasn't one at this rest stop.

"Go behind the station wagon," Mom said softly. "Just hurry before someone sees you."

"What?" I whispered back. "I can't do that!"

Seeing my hesitation, Mom sleepily grabbed a blanket, stumbled to the back of the station wagon, and held it up like a curtain. Looking around to see if anyone could see me, I gave in and, with a sigh, I did what I had to do. When I was finished, Mom told Michael to do the same. Although I don't think he cared who might be watching him, 'cause he would whip it out anywhere and just pee. Then it was Mia's

92

turn, and finally, Mom handed me the blanket so she could have her turn.

It wasn't like I'd never peed outside before—Brownie and I used to roam the farm all the time, and finding a bush or a tree was second nature. But this felt different. There were so many people around, and they all seemed to know exactly what we were doing. I caught sight of another mother doing the same thing behind her vehicle. My face burned with embarrassment.

I wasn't sure why it felt so awkward, but it did. Eventually, I'd grow used to moments like this as we traveled across the country. But in that quiet, misty morning at the rest stop, it felt like the most uncomfortable thing in the world.

As everyone slowly woke up and began mingling, Dad and the other drivers were discussing the drive ahead. It was decided that since we had leftover sandwich supplies, anyone who was hungry could eat that for breakfast. The plan was to head to Duchesne, about two hours away, where we'd stop and eat a real meal. Dad was anxious to get there—he'd promised Murphy they'd arrive yesterday and hadn't been able to call to explain the delay. He was sure Murphy was worried.

Dad clapped his hands together, signaling it was time to move. "Let's pack up and get on the road. Eat quickly or in your car. Next stop, Duchesne!"

With that, everyone began gathering their things, packing up blankets, and preparing for the next stretch of the journey. The quiet of the morning faded as engines roared to life, and we were back on the road once again.

This new morning felt exciting. We were almost to our destination, and I was eager to see this place. So far, Utah didn't look too different from where we had come from. There were some mountains, but otherwise, it was dry and hot—nothing new there. But as we continued north, the landscape began to change. The road wound through canyons and mountains covered with tall trees. It was magnificent. The air was cooler, and a light mist clung to the mountain tops. I couldn't stop staring out the window.

The highway cut through the mountains in a way that reminded me of driving through the Grapevine in California. The difference here was the little river that followed the road, winding alongside us. I saw a sign that said "Provo River." In some spots, the river was narrow and rushed over rocks, while in others, it widened into calm pools. As we drove deeper into the mountains, the trees grew taller and denser, their branches forming a canopy over the mountains. It was the most beautiful scenery I had ever seen.

You could see where road crews had carved into the mountainside to make space for the highway. The exposed rock and jagged edges told a story of disruption, and it made me feel a little sad. I couldn't help but think about the animals that might have lost their homes when the mountain was cut away. Why did they have to do that? I had seen similar scars on the land before, traveling over the Grapevine, and the feeling was always the same—a quiet sense of loss mixed with wonder at the road stretching ahead.

Sharp turns appeared suddenly, making the drive feel treacherous. Dad's voice broke the silence. "It's going to take us longer than I thought to get through these mountains with these trucks."

I couldn't tell if he was worried, but his tone made my stomach knot. A memory flashed in my mind—driving through the Grapevine when a big truck nearly hit us. Dad slowed down considerably, and Mom turned in her seat to remind Michael and Mia to stay seated. Her eyes kept darting to the back seat, making sure we all stayed seated.

The tension in the car was palpable. Dad kept checking the rearview mirror, his eyes flicking between the convoy and the winding road ahead. I could feel my heart pounding in my chest as the weight of the moment settled on me. The beauty of the mountains was still there, but now it felt overshadowed by a thick layer of anxiety.

My anxiety reached a new peak when, all of a sudden, we were driving through a tunnel cut into the mountain. I had never been in a tunnel before, and it was both terrifying and exciting. The eerie sound of the engine echoed off the tunnel walls, amplifying every noise. But just as quickly as it began, the tunnel ended, and we emerged back into the daylight. The sun was up and shining, but its light was hidden behind the towering mountains and thick trees.

Traffic seemed heavier, though I suspected it was just our convoy moving so slowly. Dad wasn't taking any chances—he kept the speed steady at around forty miles an hour. As cars passed us, I noticed people staring, and I suddenly felt out of place in this unfamiliar world.

Despite the breathtaking scenery around us, my anxiety and nervousness made it hard for me to fully appreciate the beauty. This feeling would return many times throughout my childhood, with every move we made. No matter where we went, I would always feel slightly out of place.

As we wound our way through the mountains, I noticed the road had begun a steady descent. The dense trees that had surrounded us earlier were becoming sparser, giving way to open stretches of grass. Though the mountains still loomed around us, the trees now appeared in clusters, separated by wide, empty spaces.

Dad eased off the gas, driving even more cautiously as he navigated each curve, his eyes flicking to the rearview mirror to check on the trucks trailing behind us. There were no houses or businesses in sight—just the winding road and the occasional road sign.

The farther downhill we traveled, the fewer trees there were, replaced by more expansive open spaces. Then, out of nowhere, I spotted a sign: Deer Creek.

Wait… what? Were we back in California?

Before I could make sense of it, a massive body of water came into view—Deer Creek Dam and Reservoir. Instantly, a wave of nostalgia hit me. The name Deer Creek brought back a flood of memories of me and Brownie.

Mom's voice broke the silence. "Would you look at that, Sonny? The same name as the creek by your mom's place."

Dad raised an eyebrow. "That's strange, isn't it? What are the odds that both places would share the same name?"

I couldn't stop staring at the reservoir. I stretched as far as I could, craning my neck to catch a better view of the dam and the lake. But the moment passed too quickly, the scene slipping away as we continued down the road. I leaned back in my seat, my mind drifting to Brownie and what it would be like to walk around this lake with him by my side.

Brownie had always loved the water—every trip to Deer Creek was an adventure for him. The moment we'd arrive, he'd take off running, leaping straight into the water without hesitation. I'd follow close behind, laughing as he splashed around, barking at tadpoles darting beneath the surface.

One memory stood out, clear as day. Brownie had jumped in a little too far once, and as he tried to swim back to shore, I could see the panic in his eyes. My heart stopped—I didn't think he was going to make it. Without a second thought, I jumped in after him, swimming out and scooping him up in my arms. We made it back to the shore, both of us exhausted and shaken.

I think it scared him just as much as it scared me because, after that day, Brownie was more cautious. He'd still jump in, but only from the safety of the beach and never too far out. We had both learned our lesson that day.

The memory left a bittersweet ache in my chest, but I couldn't help smiling. Brownie would've loved this lake—so much space, so much water, and so many tadpoles to chase.

We continued down the mountain pass, and soon, the trees

disappeared almost entirely, leaving behind wide-open spaces and rugged mountains dotted with small, scattered shrubs. A sign caught my eye: "Hills Block View." The warning made my stomach tighten. Dad's knuckles were still white on the steering wheel, and he kept glancing in the rearview mirror, his focus sharp.

The farther we traveled, the fewer shrubs we saw until the landscape stretched out in arid, desert-like emptiness, with the mountains standing tall in the distance. But then, almost without warning, the mountains opened up into a stunning green valley. A small town nestled below, surrounded by fields dotted with giant irrigation wheels spraying water in gentle arcs.

It felt familiar—like Central California, where we'd just come from. The scene was breathtaking, but it passed quickly. Before long, we were climbing back into the mountains, and the landscape transformed again, this time lush and green, with thick clusters of trees.

Then, another body of water appeared, larger and more expansive than the last. The highway hugged the shoreline, offering us a clear view of the sparkling surface. A sign came into view: "Strawberry Reservoir."

The name made me smile. Strawberries? I wondered if they actually grew them here. Why else would they name it that?

The drive along the reservoir was peaceful, and the sight of the water stretched out beside us felt almost magical. Dad had relaxed a little; his grip on the wheel wasn't as tight, though his eyes still flickered to the rearview mirror now and then.

We drove like that for a while, soaking in the changing scenery. Eventually, we crossed a bridge, and Dad said, "Just a few more minutes to Duchesne."

I sat up straighter, eyes fixed on the road ahead, eager to catch my first glimpse of our destination. I wasn't sure why I felt so anxious. But there I was, leaning forward, heart racing, ready to see the place we would soon call home.

Suddenly, Dad began to slow down. The change in speed limit signaled that we were entering a town. I leaned forward and spotted a sign: Strawberry River. I think they must grow strawberries around here. The road meandered gently through a valley framed by mountains with flat, mesa-like tops.

And then, there it was—the sign: Duchesne City.

Just past it, the town unfolded before us like something out of a postcard. The highway we were on seemed to double as the town's main street, and big rigs rumbled past us in the opposite direction, their engines echoing off the nearby hills.

Dad drove even slower now, and all of us craned our necks out the windows, taking in the scene. A small white church with a pointed steeple caught my eye almost immediately after we crossed the city limits. It stood quietly among clusters of small businesses and homes, each with neatly trimmed green lawns and large, welcoming trees.

Something about this little town felt warm and safe, like a place where time moved more slowly. I could already imagine myself feeling happy here.

Near the edge of town, there was a large, empty dirt lot. Dad steered into it, and like clockwork, the convoy of trucks followed, each massive vibrator truck pulling in and lining up with precision, the family cars trailing close behind.

Dad put the car in park and said, "Sit here. I'll be right back."

Through the dusty windshield, I saw Rico jump down from his truck and walk toward Dad. They spoke briefly. Dad was gesturing toward a payphone nearby before heading in that direction, probably to call Murphy and check in.

I stayed in the back seat, my window rolled down, watching the quiet bustle around me. The other families did the same; their kids were hanging out of car windows and looking around with wide eyes.

Mom handed Michael and Mia half a sandwich she'd been keeping hidden—a small peace offering to keep them quiet. The smell of the warm lunch meat filled the car, and I leaned back against the seat, taking it all in.

The sky was wide and blue above us, the mountains standing guard in the distance, and the little town of Duchesne felt like the beginning of something new, something special.

It didn't take long for Dad to finish his phone call. He walked over to the drivers who had gathered in front of our station wagon. They spoke briefly, their conversation quick and focused. After a few minutes, everyone returned to their trucks, and Dad slid back into the driver's seat.

"Murphy said there's an industrial district on the edge of town where trailers were ready for us," he explained.

Without wasting time, we headed in that direction. The drive took all of five minutes before Dad pulled into a makeshift trailer park. The convoy of trucks followed, each one carefully maneuvering off the road and into designated spots.

An elderly man emerged from a small trailer and walked toward us as Dad stepped out of the car. They shook hands, exchanged a few words, and then the man gestured for Dad to follow him back to his trailer.

I stayed in the backseat, surrounded by the buzz of activity as families began stepping out of their cars and trucks. Kids stretched their legs, and moms unpacked small bags of food and drinks.

Amid the crowd, a box truck pulled into the lot. Its engine rumbled past us as it carefully navigated around our cars and trucks onto the narrow dirt road that ran through the trailer park. The driver parked, hopped out, and opened the back of the truck.

Almost instantly, children swarmed around him, each holding a bag—some plastic, others looking like old pillowcases or makeshift sacks. The scene felt chaotic yet strangely organized.

Mom, noticing the sudden flurry of movement in that direction, leaned forward and asked, "What's going on here?"

Her voice held a mix of curiosity and concern as we both watched the scene unfold in front of us.

Mom and I sat glued to the scene unfolding before us. The man in the box truck took a bag from each child, emptied it into a bin, and hooked the bin onto a small scale in the back of his truck. He would then hand the child a few coins. One by one, the kids scurried away, clutching their money and racing toward the small store on the north side of the trailer park.

Moments later, they emerged from the store with sodas, candy, and ice cream in hand, their faces lit up with pure joy.

Mom squinted, her voice low with curiosity. "What is he getting from those children? Why is he giving them money?"

I shrugged, just as puzzled. But Mom kept watching the man intently. After a few more transactions, her face lit up with realization.

"Oh, I get it! He collects cans! The children must be bringing him aluminum cans, and he's paying them for it. That's pretty smart of him!"

Her words sparked something in me. My dad was a beer drinker—he had plenty of cans every night. I could do this too! My mind raced with excitement as I imagined gathering up all those cans, bringing them to the man, and walking away with my own money.

While my imagination spun with possibilities, Dad reappeared from the small office trailer, a handful of keys jangling in his grip. He walked from driver to driver, handing out a key to each one, before approaching Mom's window.

"Here's the key to our trailer," he said, handing it to Mom. "It's the first one past the office."

"Thank God!" she exclaimed with excitement. Without skipping a beat, she turned around in her seat, her eyes sparkling as she called out to us kids, "Come on, let's go check out our new home!"

Mom wasted no time, clutching the key and walking briskly toward our temporary home. The trailer was hidden behind a large, bushy pomegranate tree, its branches heavy with deep red fruit. We followed closely behind her, nearly stumbling into her when she stopped abruptly.

Mom stared at the trailer, her mouth falling open in disbelief. It wasn't a house trailer—it was a small travel trailer, with barely enough room for one person, let alone a family.

Michael took off running under the covered carport, while Mom turned on her heels and marched back to Dad, holding the key up like it was evidence in a courtroom. She yelled at me, "Watch the kids!" Then you could hear her from across the gravel drive, "Sonny, this isn't going to work. That trailer is entirely too small for us."

Dad sighed, his voice calm but firm. "This is only temporary until we can find better housing. The town is in the middle of an oil boom, and housing is nearly impossible to come by. We were lucky to get these trailers for everyone."

I looked around and noticed the same look on the faces of the other families as they walked up to their trailers—disappointment, worry, and exhaustion. It was clear that no one thought these tiny trailers would be enough.

Dad raised his voice slightly, trying to reassure everyone. "This is just for now. Bear with me until we can find something more suitable."

In the early 1970s, there weren't major hotels or motels scattered across small towns like Duchesne. With a population of around 10,000 to 12,000 people, half of whom were oil field workers, finding a roof over your head was a blessing, no matter how small it was.

Dad would repeat this sentiment many times throughout my childhood as we moved from one boomtown to another. I eventually learned to roll with it, to accept each new place as it came. But Mom? She never stopped complaining. And in that moment, standing in front of the tiny trailer with a pomegranate bush at its side, I could already tell she was going to have a lot to say about this arrangement.

She came stomping back over to the travel trailer, deeply frustrated. I'm sure she was tired too. I thought the little trailer was cute. The travel trailer was small and weathered, with faded white and turquoise paint peeling in spots, hinting at better days gone by. Rust crept along the edges of the wheel wells, and the aluminum siding bore a few dents and scratches, each telling a story of long miles traveled and campsites visited. The single door creaked a little on its hinges, and the screen door had a patch hastily fixed with duct tape.

Inside, the charm was undeniable. The narrow space was cozy and clean, with mismatched curtains hanging over small windows that let in warm sunlight. The dinette booth, covered in vinyl that was cracked in a few places, still felt inviting. A compact kitchenette featured an old stove and a mini-fridge, both a little scuffed but still functional. The sleeping area at the back was tucked under a curved window, with a colorful handmade quilt spread neatly over the mattress.

It smelled faintly of pine cleaner and something sweet, maybe from a long-ago batch of cookies baked in the tiny oven. A couple of landscape photos and a string of fairy lights gave it a personal, homey touch. Despite its worn appearance, the trailer had a certain scrappy charm—a reminder that even the humblest spaces could still feel warm, welcoming, and full of character.

But I don't think Mom saw the trailer the same way I did. She immediately started complaining about the cramped space, the tiny fridge, and the little stove she clearly didn't trust. She didn't care for the mismatched photos on the walls or the fairy lights strung along the window. The air inside was thick and stuffy, and her face was turning redder by the minute.

With a sharp sigh, she threw up her hands and stomped back outside. Standing under the tiny carport, she grabbed an old newspaper left on the counter and started fanning herself furiously. She stayed there for a while, her face tight with frustration, before finally calling out, "Let's clean this place up before we put any of our stuff inside!"

I sprinted to the station wagon and grabbed a couple of rags while Mom went back inside to check if there was hot running water and if the toilet worked. We spent the next hour scrubbing every surface, wiping down counters, and airing out the trailer. Mom pulled all the bedding out and piled it under the carport, muttering under her breath as she worked.

Dad eventually wandered over after helping everyone else settle in. He tried talking to Mom, but she barely acknowledged him, her silence louder than any argument. I could tell she was angry, and I knew this wasn't something she was going to let go of anytime soon.

After a while, Dad gave up trying to talk to her. With a sigh, he said he was going to find us something to eat and needed to call Murphy. That's when Mom snapped, "Oh yeah? Well, be sure to thank Murphy for these wonderful accommodations!" Dad didn't say another word—he just turned around and walked away.

We kept cleaning until the trailer felt fresh and smelled better. Once we were done, we hauled all the bedding back inside. Mom had given Michael and Mia some crayons and paper to keep them occupied while we worked. They sat quietly at the little table, scribbling away, which was unusual but honestly a relief.

When the cleaning was done, Mom did her best to make the cramped space feel like home. She decided that she and Dad would sleep in the back with Michael, while Mia and I would share the table that folded down into a bed. During the day, we'd turn it back into a table where we could sit and eat together.

Before long, Dad returned with hamburgers from a small café in

103

town. He told Mom she could walk to the little store on Main Street tomorrow—it wasn't far, which was good since Mom didn't drive. She just nodded and said, "Okay." I could tell she was exhausted.

I took my burger and stepped outside to eat under the carport. It was stiflingly hot inside the trailer, but out here, sitting close to the pomegranate bush, the air smelled cool and sweet. I felt peaceful, nibbling on my burger in the quiet shade. For a little while, everything felt still, and I was happy just to sit there, all by myself.

I sat next to the pomegranate bush for a long time after finishing my burger. From where I was, I could see all the way down the gravel driveway, past the other trailers. The crew was scattered about— parents unloading their cars, kids running around, and a few playing on the small playground next to the little country store.

The playground had a couple of swings, a metal slide that glinted in the sun, and an old teeter-totter that looked warped and dry-rotted. Despite the worn-out equipment, the grass surrounding it was surprisingly green. That's when the urge hit me—I wanted to take off my shoes and feel the cool ground beneath my feet.

I kicked off my black-and-white tennis shoes, carefully tucking my socks inside them. Losing those socks wasn't an option; if I did, Mom would kill me.

I pressed my toes into the gravel, wiggling them deeper under the smooth, cool stones. The sensation was oddly comforting, almost magical. A soft breeze rustled through the pomegranate bush beside me, carrying its faint, sweet scent. The cool gravel under my toes, the soft rustling leaves, and the gentle breeze made everything feel still and peaceful. It was such a simple moment, but it felt wonderful.

I got to sit there playing with the cool gravel for what felt like a long time, which was surprising—Mom usually would've hollered at me by now to help with something. Eventually, Michael and Mia came bouncing out of the little trailer, with Dad following close behind. He announced that he had a meeting with the drivers. Murphy had given him the work details, and they'd be heading out first thing in the morning to get the trucks moving.

Mom stepped out behind him and spotted me with my toes still buried in the gravel. "What are you doing?" she asked.

"The stones are nice and cool," I replied.

That was all Michael and Mia needed to hear—they immediately kicked off their shoes and socks to join me. Mom scooped up their shoes and socks, still talking to Dad as they walked to the end of the carport.

Michael started tossing rocks, earning a quick swat on the butt from Mom, though it didn't stop him. It wasn't until Dad snapped his fingers sharply that Michael froze, dropped the rock, and went back to quietly stacking stones into little piles before knocking them over again. Meanwhile, Mia had already lost interest in the gravel and was clinging to Mom's skirt, as usual.

"I'll be back," Dad said before walking off.

Mom turned back to me and said, "Let's unpack what we can." And just like that, my peaceful moment was over. I sighed, put my socks and shoes back on, and headed to the station wagon to start hauling things inside.

The rest of the day was a blur of unpacking, repacking what wouldn't fit, and trying again. By the time the sun dipped below the horizon, I was bone-tired. Dad returned with a small bag of groceries, and Mom got to work making spaghetti on the little stove.

We all sat around the tiny table, eating the warm pasta filling our bellies. After dinner, Mom made up the bed on the table for Mia and me. The moment my head hit the pillow, I was out—full, tired, and completely done for the day.

Chapter 5:
Carol

The next morning, I woke to the sound of the small travel trailer's metallic door creaking open, followed by the sharp slam of the screen door. Dad was already up and out, his movements breaking the fragile stillness of the early morning. I lay there for a few minutes, cocooned in the thin blanket, staring at the soft light filtering through the small window. Outside, I could hear the gravel crunching as Dad drove away, and faint voices of children echoed somewhere in the distance. The sun was just beginning to rise, painting the sky with hues of pale gold and pink.

Mom's rustling in the tiny kitchenette broke my sleepy spell. Without turning around, she said, "We need to go to the grocery store this morning. Oh, and I need to find a laundromat. I think I saw one nearby, close to that Mormon church."

Before long, Michael and Mia were awake, their sleepy faces still creased from the pillows. We dressed quickly, excitement bubbling up as we prepared to explore this unfamiliar place. Stepping outside, I paused by the vibrant pomegranate bush growing next to the trailer. Its deep red flowers gave off a sweet yet tangy scent that made me smile. It was such a small thing, but it felt magical, like the world was offering me a secret moment of happiness. How did she know that was a Mormon church? All churches looked the same to me.

Following Dad's directions, we made our way down the narrow road towards the small grocery store. The houses we passed had lush green lawns, and one stood out—a modest brick building with a tall steeple. "That's a Mormon church," Mom said thoughtfully. "I wonder if that's the only church in town. It would be nice to find a Baptist one."

Just one block later, there it was—a small Baptist church with white siding and stained-glass windows glowing in the morning sun. Mom stopped in her tracks, a look of relief crossing her face. As if on cue, the church doors opened, and out stepped a young woman with a warm smile and honey-colored hair.

"Hello there! I'm Ann Hathaway," she said brightly while waving. "Are you here for Vacation Bible School? It starts in just a few weeks!"

Before I knew it, Mom and Ms. Hathaway were deep in conversation. Mom explained how we'd just arrived from California, how she was looking for something to keep us busy during the summer, and how Vacation Bible School sounded perfect.

Ms. Hathaway was around twenty-eight or twenty-nine, with honey-blonde hair pulled back into a neat ponytail, the kind that stayed in place no matter how busy her day got. She had a calm, steady presence—soft-spoken but confident, with eyes that lit up when she talked about books or helping others.

She was originally from Salt Lake City and had grown up in a tight-knit family where Sunday dinners and community service were part of the rhythm of life. That upbringing shaped her deeply, she told Mom. Now, she works full-time for the Baptist church, coordinating youth programs and outreach events with a quiet passion. Her days were long, often spilling into evenings spent tutoring students who needed a little extra help, so if any of Mom's kids needed any help, she would be glad to help out. She believed every child deserved a shot, and she made sure they got it, whether they could afford it or not.

She was single by choice, she said. Her life was filled with purpose and people, but there was not much room for dating. She spoke with intention, saying that she filled her time with things that mattered: teaching, listening, and showing up. She wasn't flashy, but she was energetic.

By the look on Mom's face, she was thrilled. "This is perfect!" she exclaimed. "Vacation Bible School will keep them busy, out of trouble, and close to God."

Ms. Hathaway nodded kindly. She and Mom spoke about the start date and a few other things, which I didn't care about, so I stopped paying attention.

I did hear her say that Michael and Mia would be in one class together, and I, being older, would be stuck in a different one. Alone. With strangers. She was a typical mom, always signing me up for things without asking how I felt about any of them.

As we walked away from the church, the sun was climbing higher in the sky. I kicked at a loose stone in the gravel and sighed. A summer in a strange town, filled with strange people, and now Vacation Bible School? Great.

We walked about two more blocks and found the small grocery store. It looked just as one would imagine a small-town market would: handwritten signs taped to big glass windows, a man sweeping the front walkway, and a modest but varied selection of items visible through the glass. As we stepped inside, Mom said firmly, "Keep an eye on your brother." I grabbed Michael's hand, knowing full well he was seconds away from making a run for it. Mia, on the other hand, clung to Mom's side like her life depended on it.

Mom grabbed a cart by the door and was greeted by an older woman working the register. "Welcome to Allen's! Let us know if you need any help."

People here sure were friendly. Back in L.A., you could spend an hour in a grocery store without speaking to a single person. It felt different here, and apparently, Mom liked it because she smiled and said, "Thank you so much. We just arrived from California."

I winced. Did she have to announce it every time? Everyone probably already knew we were strangers, but hearing her say it out loud made me squirm.

We wandered down the narrow aisles as Mom picked out a few essentials—some bread, milk, and a box of cereal. Michael kept trying to pull away until Mom finally hoisted him into the basket. She handed him a pack of crackers she had grabbed off a shelf, and for the moment, he was content.

"I'm sure he's hungry," Mom said absentmindedly.

Come to think of it, I was hungry too. But I kept quiet and followed along as we made our way to the register. Mom exchanged a few words with the cashier, but I wasn't paying attention. Instead, I watched the elderly man bagging our groceries. He looked ancient— maybe a hundred years old—and he reminded me of the man I'd seen driving the box truck the day before.

As he placed glass Coke bottles into a bag, he glanced at me and said, "If you bring these bottles back here, I'll give you five cents for each one."

I nodded quickly. "I will."

"What's your name?" he asked.

I hesitated, glanced at Mom, who was deep in conversation with the cashier, and blurted out, "Carol."

I don't know why I lied. Maybe it was a leftover sense of stranger danger. But Harold—that was his name, Harold—smiled warmly.

"Nice to meet you, Carol. Are you staying over at the trailer park a few blocks away?"

My stomach twisted slightly. Before I could answer, Mom noticed the conversation. She turned toward him and said, "Yes, we are. Didn't I see you there yesterday, collecting cans from the children?"

Harold nodded, his wrinkled face lighting up. The cashier chimed in, "That's Harold. He collects all kinds of things around town."

Harold explained, "Twice a week, I drive through the trailer park and collect cans from the kids. I give them a little money—enough for candy or a Coke. Helps me out, and it makes them happy."

Then he turned back to me and said, "I'll be by next Thursday. If you have any cans around your place, bring them out."

I spoke up quickly, almost too quickly. "I'll bring you some cans for sure."

I didn't want him to call me by my fake name in front of Mom. Thankfully, he didn't.

Mom took the bags, and I took Michael's hand as we headed back out onto the gravel road. On the walk back, Mom said, "You can collect all of Dad's cans, but you'll need to share the money with Michael and Mia. That's the rule."

It never failed. I always had to share everything with those two.

The sun had climbed higher, and the day was heating up. The trailer park came into view, and the distant sound of kids playing floated on the warm breeze. For now, the promise of collecting cans and earning a little money sparked a flicker of excitement in me. Maybe this summer wouldn't be so bad after all.

We returned to the small trailer and unloaded our few groceries. Mom moved with quiet focus, searching for space to tuck everything away in the cramped kitchenette. Trailer space was sparse, but she was resourceful, making every inch count. Once the groceries were stowed, she grabbed a pillow from one of the beds, stripped off the pillowcase, and began stuffing it with dirty clothes.

I guessed that meant we were heading to the laundromat. That's what she and the cashier had been talking about because Mom said, "The cashier told me where to find a laundromat, so let's get some of these clothes washed up."

She pulled a handful of coins from her purse, the metallic clink filling the quiet trailer, and motioned for us to follow her out the door.

As we walked through the trailer park, I noticed kids scattered around, their laughter and shouts filling the warm afternoon air. Some played catch on the gravel driveway, while others took turns swinging high on a rusty metal swing set. It looked fun, free, and easy in a way that made me wish to join them.

"Mom, can I stay here? Please? I promise I'll stay right here," I asked, hope rising in my voice.

But Mom didn't even slow her pace as she shot back a firm, "Absolutely not."

"Oh, and by the way, no one, and I mean no one, is allowed by the creek!" Mom said firmly.

Mom hated water. She had almost drowned in the Pacific Ocean when she was a small child. One of her brothers pulled her by the hair of the head from the riptide and barely saved her. Since then, she hasn't wanted us around water at all. I didn't think she knew about Deer Creek back home at Grandma's, but maybe she did. Or perhaps she was just being cautious since the Strawberry River in Duchesne was so close you could hear the water running over the rocks late at night.

Later in life, after another move, Mom would make all of us take swimming lessons. I got good at swimming, and so did my brother, but my sister didn't like the water. She had seen my little brother almost drown at Castaic Lake in California, and since then, she didn't even want to take baths. She was a weird little kid.

I groaned and whined a little, hoping she might change her mind and let me stay behind to play, but then she turned and gave me a look—one sharp glance that said everything without a word. I stopped complaining immediately.

It wasn't Mom I was afraid of. It was Dad. If I pushed too hard and upset Mom, she'd tell Dad, and that was a line I never wanted to cross. You didn't make Dad mad.

I sighed and trudged along behind her, my shoes kicking up small clouds of dust from the gravel path. The laundromat awaited, but my mind stayed back with those kids on the swings and the sound of their carefree laughter drifting through the air.

We walked forever, but I guess it wasn't really that long since the town was so tiny. It just felt long because it was so hot, and the laundry was so heavy. When we finally found the laundromat, Mom started loading up the washers, and I begrudgingly helped.

The laundromat was gross, hot, stuffy, and way too loud. A couple of other women were there, and some little kids were running around, shrieking and laughing.

I was melting inside, so I asked Mom if I could wait outside, and she said okay. As soon as I opened the door, a rush of cooler air hit me. Finally! I plopped down on the ground right in front of the big windows, sitting in the shade with nothing to do.

Bored, my mind drifted back to Grandma's farm and Brownie. Brownie would have loved it here. I wished more than anything that I had him with me instead of my super annoying little brother and sister.

I thought about how I really didn't want to leave L.A. when we moved to Grandma's house in Central California. And now we were in Utah. Utah! It felt like forever since we left L.A., but at the same time, it also felt like it all happened so fast.

I sat there, staring out at the empty street, my arms wrapped around my knees. My mind drifted back to all the times Brownie and I ran up and down the red dirt road behind Grandma's house. The way his paws kicked up dust, the way he'd race ahead of me, then turn back, tongue lolling, waiting for me to catch up. I could almost hear his bark echoing in the quiet.

I thought about Deer Creek Pond, the way the water felt when I jumped in on a hot day—cool and smooth, like slipping into a secret world. I thought about the cherry trees, the walnut orchard, the cotton fields stretching out forever, their fluffy white tops swaying in the wind. I missed it all so much it hurt.

And before that, before Grandma's house, there was L.A. The busy streets, the cars honking, the voices of my friends calling my name as we played. I missed that, too. The noise. The people. The way everything felt alive. I didn't want to leave back then, just like I didn't want to leave Grandma's. But no one ever asked what I wanted.

Then I thought about something else—something that made my heart beat a little faster. That man at the grocery store, Harold. Why had I told him my name was Carol? I didn't even know a Carol. The name just tumbled out of my mouth like it had been waiting there all along.

But the thing was—he believed me.

A little thrill ran through me. No one here knew my real name. No one would know unless I told them. And right then, sitting alone outside that hot, stuffy laundromat, I decided—if anyone in this town asked my name, I was going to say Carol. The thought gave me a sense of power, although I wasn't sure why.

I sat outside, kicking at the dusty ground, watching the world go by for what felt like forever. A couple of cars rolled past, and a dog trotted down the street like he had important business to take care of. Every now and then, I peeked through the big glass window of the laundromat, watching the clothes spin in the dryers like a tornado of socks and T-shirts.

Finally, Mom pushed open the laundromat door with her hip and called, "Come help me fold."

I groaned but got up anyway, brushing the dust off my shorts. The moment I stepped back inside, the thick, hot air wrapped around me like a blanket I did not want. The place smelled like soap and warm fabric, with a hint of something musty, like old pennies. The machines were huge and clunky, their paint chipped away in places. The tile floor was cracked, and some of the laundry baskets were missing wheels, so people had to drag them around like stubborn mules. But it got the job done, I guess.

I pulled a hot T-shirt out of the basket and folded it fast, pretending it was straight out of the oven. "Careful, it's piping hot!" I said in my most dramatic voice, making Mom laugh. We folded the rest of the clothes as quickly as we could, stuffing everything into pillowcases.

Once we had everything ready to go, we stepped outside, and finally, we had fresh air again! As we headed back to the little trailer park, I started thinking, maybe the kids there would want to play when we got back. I really hoped so. Anything was better than sitting around being bored all day.

The walk back to the trailer park was long and dusty, the heat pressing down like a heavy blanket. I kicked at a rock, watching it bounce along the cracked pavement, when suddenly a rusty old truck rumbled up beside us. Harold.

He leaned out the window, squinting at us through the glare. "Y'all need a ride?"

Mom didn't even hesitate. She pulled my little brother up higher on her hip and gave him the kind of polite-but-firm smile that meant absolutely not. "No, thank you," she said, her voice smooth but clipped.

Harold nodded, then turned his gaze to me. "Don't forget, next Thursday."

I swallowed hard and nodded back, feeling a strange little thrill shoot through me.

"Well, y'all have a nice day," he said, tipping his hat before rolling off down the road in a cloud of dust and exhaust.

Mom's face was flushed, but I couldn't tell if it was the heat or something else. She adjusted my brother on her hip and started walking faster, her sandals slapping against the pavement. I matched her pace, wondering why she seemed so rattled.

By the time we got back to the trailer park, my shirt was sticking to my back, and I was dying for something cold. We unloaded the clothes as fast as we could, and Mom handed each of us a soda. The bottle was so cold it felt like heaven against my sweaty palms.

"Drink it under the carport," she said, already heading inside. Then, over her shoulder—of course—she yelled, "Watch your brother and sister!"

I sighed. Every. Single. Time.

Michael and Mia, the little wild animals that they were, took off running across the gravel driveway. I leaned against one of the support beams of the carport, sipping my soda and watching them. I should have told them to slow down, but I didn't. I just knew one of them was going to fall and get hurt, but honestly, I figured they needed to learn.

And sure enough—bam! Mia's foot slid on the gravel, and she hit the ground hard, scraping her knee. Blood trickled down her leg, and the moment she saw it, she let out a wail that could have shattered glass.

Here came Mom, sprinting out of the trailer, already scolding before she even saw what had happened. And, of course, somehow, it was my fault.

I got yelled at, but it didn't bother me. Not today. Because for the first time in my life, I felt something shift—I felt power in my own hands. I wasn't just someone's kid or the quiet one who followed orders. I had a secret name now, one that belonged only to me, a name that no one in this town could trace. And I had a job waiting. My own job. I was finally going to earn money that was mine, not handed down, not borrowed, not controlled. Maybe I'd share a little with Michael and Mia, maybe I wouldn't. But that choice would be mine. Even letting Mia fall—it wasn't out of carelessness. It was a test. I needed to know if I could handle the weight of decisions and if I could live with the consequences. And I could. No one noticed. No one questioned. That's when I knew: I had crossed into a new kind of freedom.

Something had shifted in me. I didn't know where this new bravery came from, but I liked it. I had always been the responsible one, always looking after my little brother and sister while they got to cry and whine and have people fuss over them. They were adorable, with their blonde hair and big blue eyes, while I was just... me. A redheaded, freckle-faced, awkward thing.

People never called me adorable. They just looked at me and said, "Oh my! What red hair you have!" like I was some kind of circus act.

Well, not anymore. Not here. No one in this town knew who I was, so I was going to be whoever I wanted to be. A tough, independent kid. Someone nobody messed with.

Let them try and make fun of my freckles and red hair.

It didn't matter anyway. We probably wouldn't be in this town for very long before we had to move again.

Mom took Mia inside to clean her up and calm her down, leaving me outside with Michael. Watch him and make sure he doesn't fall, she hollered.

Wouldn't that be something? What if he went running around again and he fell too? I smirked at the thought. Not because I wanted him to get hurt—of course not—but because maybe, just maybe, they'd both learn a lesson. Wow. Was I actually thinking like a mean person?

Before I could think too much about it, a couple of kids walked up to the carport. They were part of our crew, but I didn't know them well. The older boy, Mario, looked about my age, maybe a little older. The younger one clung to his side like a shadow.

"Hey," Mario said, kicking at a rock. "We're looking for cans to sell to the old man. You guys got any cans?"

I folded my arms and tilted my chin up a little. "I told Harold I'd give him some cans on Thursday," I said, making sure to say his name like it was no big deal, like I knew things.

116

Mario raised an eyebrow. "Oh, you know Harold?"

"Yeah," I said smoothly. "Met him at the grocery store this morning." Then, without even thinking, I added, "Hi, I'm Carol. Maybe we could look for cans together."

It rolled off my tongue so easily, like I'd been Carol my whole life.

Mario shrugged. "Cool. This is my little brother, Jesús. My mom makes me drag him everywhere."

I perked up. "Oh wow! Same. I have to drag my little brother and sister everywhere, too." Did I just find a kindred spirit?

Right then, the trailer door creaked open, and out walked Mom, Mia trailing behind her like a little lost puppy. As always, Mia stayed behind Mom, peeking out like she was afraid of the world.

Mom looked at Mario and Jesús, then at me. "Who are these little guys?"

Mario launched into his introduction again, telling her his mom's name.

"Oh yeah!" Mom nodded. "I know your mother!"

I bit my tongue. That was a lie. Mom barely talked to anyone, let alone Mario's mom. But whatever. If I could lie, I guess Mom could, too. Maybe if I didn't call her out on it, she wouldn't be mad when she eventually found out I had a brand-new name.

I cleared my throat. "Mom, can I go with Mario and Jesús down the gravel road to the swings?"

I expected her to say no, but to my surprise, she said, "Yes, but only until the sun starts going down."

Yes! Finally, some freedom!

But then, of course, she had to ruin it.

"Oh, and take your little brother."

Oh, for Christ's sake.

I huffed, but whatever. Maybe Michael could run off with Jesús, and I wouldn't have to babysit him too much.

So off we went to the small playground in the trailer park. On the way, I turned to Mario and asked, "Hey, I'm gonna get all the cans I can from my dad. Does your dad drink a lot too?"

Mario nodded. He said his dad and his uncle drank every night after work, and by the time Harold came around on Thursday, they would have a ton of cans saved up.

I only had one dad and no uncle, so I started thinking—maybe I could team up with Mario. If we pooled our cans together and split the money, maybe Mario wouldn't know the difference.

But I had more ideas, too. I was already planning to walk down the gravel road and check the trash bins for cans. I was determined to find as many as possible. Still, I kept that part to myself. No need to give Mario too many of my secrets—he might try to get there before I do.

We played on the swings and chased each other around the little playground with the other trailer park kids until the sun started to dip low in the sky. The metal slide had finally cooled down enough to use, and someone had found a half-deflated ball, so we kicked it around until it rolled under a bush, and nobody felt like crawling after it. I caught glimpses of Mom here and there—her head peeking out from behind the pomegranate bush by our trailer, just checking in, making sure we were okay, but letting us have our freedom.

As soon as the sun disappeared completely and the shadows got long and thick, I grabbed my little brother's hand and started walking back toward our trailer. "Night, Mario! Night, Jesus!" I called out over my shoulder. They waved, still playing. Other kids were heading home too, their voices echoing through the night—laughing, calling

118

out to siblings, feet slapping against the worn gravel paths.

By the time I climbed into bed, the air was cooler, and the sky outside had turned deep blue, almost black. I stared at the ceiling for a while, thinking about the day. About the cans. About the secret name I had chosen for myself. It was strange—just changing my name, even if no one else knew it, made me feel different. Stronger. Like I had a piece of myself that was mine alone, untouched by the rules. I didn't know exactly what it meant, but I held onto that feeling as I closed my eyes.

That night, when I fell asleep, I wasn't the same kid I had been that morning. I was someone new. Someone a little more in control.

The next morning, I shot out of bed like a rocket, fired up, and ready. I had a mission, and nothing was going to slow me down. I told Mom straight up, "I'm going through the trash to get Dad's beer cans."

Without blinking, she handed me a trash bag. Just like that. No lecture, no "take your brother" or "watch your sister." I stood there for half a second, stunned. Was this really happening? She wasn't going to stop me?

I didn't wait around to find out. I bolted through the metallic screen door like it might slam shut behind me and ruin everything. She probably thought I was just grabbing cans from our bin, but I had bigger plans. I was hitting the whole street. Every trash bin I could find.

First stop: our bin. A big, dented, metallic box half full from last night's drinking. I climbed inside like I was diving for treasure and started hurling cans out in a frenzy. Clink. Clank. Smash. When I was sure I'd scraped the bottom clean, I jumped out and stomped every single can flat, one by one, the crunch under my shoe echoing in the quiet morning air.

I stuffed them into the trash bag, tied a knot, and moved on like a machine. One bin after another. It was still early—no one was up yet. Perfect. I needed a head start before other kids caught on and tried to copy me.

Six bins in, sweat on my forehead, and my bag getting heavy, I heard it—my mom's voice cutting through the stillness, calling my name down the gravel road.

Damn.

I barely made it halfway down one side of the trailer park before she realized I'd gone. But I didn't care—I'd already made progress. And the fire inside me? It wasn't going out anytime soon.

I grabbed my full bag of cans and took off running, legs pounding the gravel, dust flying up behind me. I had to get back before Mom figured out how far I'd wandered. When I reached the trailer, I slowed to a walk, catching my breath so she wouldn't see I'd been sprinting. She was standing in the carport, squinting down the road in the opposite direction.

"Hey, what's up, Mom?" I said, trying to sound casual.

She turned and spotted the bulging trash bag in my hand. "Oh my," she said, eyebrows raised. "Your father must've drunk quite a bit last night!"

Guilt bubbled up, but I swallowed it down. "Yeah," I said, nodding. "Looks like he did."

I asked if I could check the trash bin next to ours, already bracing for the 'No' I thought was coming. She glanced down the gravel road, saw how close it was, and just said, "Sure." Then she turned and headed back inside.

I stood there frozen for a second, stunned again. She wasn't stopping me. I was on my own.

I bolted down the road, back to where I'd left off, heart pounding with excitement. When I got to the next bin, I dove right in. But halfway through, I realized—one bag wasn't going to cut it. Panic flickered. I didn't want to go back and risk Mom asking questions.

So, I got resourceful. I found a bag already full of trash, dumped the contents right there in the bin, and claimed it as my own. I didn't care how it looked—I was on a mission.

In no time, I had two bags filled with crushed beer and soda cans, each one squashed flat under my heel like a trophy. But then I noticed a few kids starting to come out of their trailers, blinking in the morning light. I couldn't let them see me—not yet.

I hustled back to our trailer, one bag in each hand, heavy and clinking with victory. I ducked behind the pomegranate bush and shoved them deep underneath, where no one would think to look. Safe.

Then I walked inside like nothing had happened, washed up, and sat down like it was just another day. But it wasn't.

I did the same thing the next day. And the next. And the day after that.

By the time Thursday came around, I had seven fat bags lined up under that bush, each one a symbol of my fire, my hustle, and my quiet rise to power.

Thursday morning, I stood under the carport, arms crossed, eyes locked on the entrance to the trailer park. I could feel the weight of the seven trash bags hidden behind the pomegranate bush like they were trophies lined up in my mind. I'd counted them twice. I knew exactly how many I had. What I didn't know was if I'd accidentally taken cans that other kids might've been counting on. Maybe they just hadn't gotten to the bins fast enough. Perhaps they never planned to. Either way, I wasn't about to give them a reason to point fingers.

If anyone accused me, I'd say it straight—my dad drank a lot, which wasn't a lie. Not the whole truth, maybe, but enough to keep them quiet. They didn't know what went on inside our trailer at night.

Just as I was running through every possible confrontation in my head, I heard it—the low rumble of a box truck coming down the road.

My heart jumped. Harold.

I moved to the edge of the carport and watched him roll in, the morning sun bouncing off his windshield. And then—he pulled right up to my trailer.

Game on.

I rushed to the bush and grabbed two heavy bags, lugging them over just as Harold hopped out and started unlocking the back of the truck. He slid the door up and pulled out his weight scale, as if it were business as usual, but not for me. This was my moment.

Suddenly, I heard the sound of feet pounding on gravel. A swarm of other kids came running toward the truck, each one dragging their small stash of cans behind them. Some had grocery bags, some had pillowcases, but none of their cans were smashed. None of them had put in the work. I stared at their clinking, bloated bags and realized— they weren't digging through bins, waking up early, or sneaking around to stay ahead. Their moms and dads were just saving cans for them inside the trailer.

That's when I knew. I had outworked them all.

So I stepped back and told Harold, "I've got a couple more bags, but you can weigh theirs first."

I set my two bags gently next to his truck tire, then leaned back and waited. Watched. The other kids huddled around, all proud of their small hauls. Let them have their turn. I wasn't worried.

When Harold finally looked over at me, he squinted and said, "Carol, right?"

"That's right," I said, standing tall. "I've got these two bags here— and five more."

His eyebrows shot up.

"I've been working hard all week," I added. "Didn't want to miss you."

I took off running, grabbing two more bags from the bush. Back and forth I went, each trip faster than the last, until all seven bags stood lined up at the back of his truck like soldiers ready for inspection.

Harold took off his hat and scratched his head, staring at the mountain of crushed aluminum. Then, without a word, he bent down and got to work, weighing every last one.

And I stood there, chest high, heart pounding—not with nerves, but with pride. I had earned every single can.

Harold weighed every single bag, one by one, scribbling the numbers down in his little flip notebook. I stood there, trying to play it cool, but my heart was racing. I watched him lick the tip of his pencil and start doing the math—adding up the weights, then multiplying by the price per pound. His lips moved silently as he worked, and I held my breath.

Then he looked up and said, "Well, Carol… that comes to twenty-two dollars."

Twenty-two dollars.

I nearly fainted right there in the dust. Twenty-two dollars! I was rich! Real money—money I had earned all by myself. Even if I gave my little brother and sister a dollar each, I'd still have twenty dollars. Twenty dollars in my own pocket. Not from chores, not from begging, not from anyone handing it over out of pity. Mine.

Harold must've seen the look on my face, because he grinned and said, "You did good, Carol. Think you can do that again next week?"

I nodded fast. "I think I can."

He handed over the cash, folded, crisp, and warm from his hand. I didn't hesitate—I slid it straight into my pocket like it was the most valuable thing I'd ever touched. He packed up his scale, rolled the truck door down with a loud clang, and waved as he climbed into the cab.

"See you next week," he called. "Keep up the great work!"

"Will do," I said, backing up, watching as his truck rumbled off down the gravel road and disappeared around the corner.

I stood there for a long moment, the breeze tugging at my shirt, dust swirling at my feet. I had done something big. Something that made me feel capable. I didn't want to run straight to Mom with the news—she'd just take the money or start asking questions. I needed a plan.

So I walked to the little corner store instead, my steps light but steady. I bought four ice-cold glass bottles of Coke and four candy bars. One for me. One each for my brother and sister. And one for Mom. It was enough to make it seem like I'd done well… but not too well.

I slipped most of the money into my left pocket and kept just two dollars in my right, the ones I'd let be seen. When I walked through the trailer door, holding the treats like a hero returning from battle, Mom looked up and said, "Oh wow! You must've done really good with those cans if you could buy everyone a Coke and some candy."

"Yup," I said with a smile. "I did. And I've even got two dollars left."

"Well," she said, almost smirking, "don't spend it all in one place."

I wasn't sure what that meant—there was only one place to spend it around here—but I laughed anyway. I felt a tiny pang of guilt for not telling her the whole truth, but it was drowned out by the pride burning in my chest.

I had worked hard. I had earned something. And for the first time, I had power in my pocket.

I spent the rest of that day playing in the park with the other kids. Mom said as long as we stayed close and kept to the park, we could play as much as we wanted—and that was fine by me. I'd managed to pull off something big: I'd made real money, made Mom smile, and even brought joy to my little brother and sister. Maybe that's what people mean when they say money buys happiness.

There was a flicker of guilt about lying to Mom, but I pushed it down. What I felt more than anything was pride. And something else, something new—power. Quiet, steady power. The kind that doesn't make a scene, but shifts the ground under your feet just enough to make you stand taller.

I kept waking up early, sneaking out while the park was still asleep, diving into trash bins, and digging for cans. One morning, I had to take my little brother with me so Mom wouldn't ask questions—I told her I was just watching him at the park. I kept him nearby, and when no one was looking, I got to work.

One day, as I was jumping out of a bin with a handful of cans, Mario caught me. He came walking over, eyebrows raised, just as I started stomping on the cans, flattening each one under my heel with a satisfying crunch.

"What are you doing?" he asked.

I looked up, a little caught off guard. Then I stood tall and said, "I'm smashing these cans for Harold. I get more cans in each bag that way."

He looked puzzled. "Smashing the cans?"

"Yeah," I said. "More cans, more money."

His eyes lit up, like the gears were turning. "You want help?"

I hesitated for a moment, then nodded. "Sure. If you help me smash the cans while I throw them out of the bin, I'll give you a cut of the money."

His grin said it all. "Alright!"

And just like that, we became a team. Every morning, we'd meet up early. I'd climb into the bins and toss the cans out, and Mario would stomp on them like it was the best game he'd ever played. Then we'd load the bags, tie them tight, and move to the next bin like a two-person army.

For the next three weeks, we didn't miss a day. I sold the cans to Harold every Thursday, gave Mario a couple of bucks, and still had enough left to buy a little something for my brother, sister, and Mom. It felt good. I was helping everyone, and no one even knew how deep it ran.

By the end of the fourth week, I had $48 stashed away—money no one knew about. My money.

Word started to spread, like things do in small places. A couple of the other trailer park kids caught wind of what Mario and I were doing and wanted in. I didn't hesitate. I told them they could each earn a couple of bucks a week if they helped. They'd jump into the bins and toss the cans out, Mario would do the stomping, and I'd bag it all up. We were like a well-oiled machine.

It never occurred to me that the grown men in the park might be drinking too much. I didn't think about their tired faces or slurred words. I just wanted more cans. I even started handing out full beers to the guys sitting around after work, hoping to keep the supply going. I thought I was being smart. Strategic.

But it all started to unravel one night when a fight broke out between a couple of the work guys, yelling, shoving, one of them bleeding from the nose. The cops showed up, and the trailer park manager came stomping over to our unit the next day.

"No more drinking in the park," he told my dad, loud enough for half the park to hear. "I don't want cops showing up every time someone gets drunk and stupid."

Just like that, the cans stopped piling up.

Our little enterprise slowed to a crawl. But I didn't forget how it felt—that rush of running things, of making something out of nothing.

That pride. That power. It was the first time in my life I'd felt like the boss of something. And I knew one thing for sure: I was just getting started.

It was the next week when Mom announced we'd be going to Bible school. Every day. For a whole week.

My stomach turned. I knew right then and there—I didn't want any part of it. I hated religion. I didn't want to sit in some stuffy room being told what to believe, being lectured about things I didn't believe in. And I wasn't going to go quietly.

I knew I wouldn't win this fight. But I wasn't going to just roll over. I had to say something. I had to let her know where I stood.

"I don't want to go to Bible school," I told her, voice firm. "I don't believe in God."

I should've stopped at the first part. I probably could've worn her down if I'd just left it at that. But I said the quiet part out loud—the part you're never supposed to say in our house.

Her eyes widened. And then it happened. She exploded.

She went into a full-blown tirade about faith, God, sin, respect, and everything else she could throw into the storm. Something about how dare I say that. From this day forward, I'd be going to church every Sunday. How I needed to learn some reverence.

I tuned most of it out. I couldn't keep up with the avalanche of words, but I knew I had struck a nerve so deep there was no coming back. Bible school was happening—no escape now.

So, Monday morning came, and Mom got us all up, dressed us, and marched us down the gravel road to the little white church with the tall steeple. She wasn't angry anymore, just dead set.

When we reached the church, other kids were already walking through the front doors. Mom pointed and told me, "Take your brother and sister in."

Ms. Hathaway stood in the doorway, smiling like this was the best part of her week, waving us in like she was welcoming us to a party.

I dragged my feet up the church steps, my brother and sister behind me. Inside, we stood there awkwardly, the cool air from the building making the place feel more serious somehow.

Ms. Hathaway pointed to a nearby room and said, "They go in there." Then she looked at me. "You can sit here on the bench with the older kids until we start."

I sat down stiffly, surrounded by faces I didn't know. I kept my eyes on the floor and waited.

I didn't want to be there. But I was. And I knew from then on that this wasn't just about one week of Bible school. This was a line in the sand. And I had just crossed it.

It wasn't long before Ms. Hathaway approached us, the older kids. There were only five of us in total. I looked around and wondered where Mario was. I guess his mom didn't make him come to Vacation Bible School.

Later in life, I'd think back to that moment and realize—maybe Mario's family was Catholic. That might've explained why he wasn't there. Of course, as a kid, I didn't really know the differences between religions, and honestly, I didn't care. But looking back, it made sense.

Ms. Hathaway told us older kids to follow her to another room down the hall. We marched single file through the church, our footsteps echoing on the tile. The room she led us to was small, tucked off to the side—and it turned out to be the church library.

She told us we could read any books we wanted while we were there. She explained that her job was to teach the younger kids, and that since we were older, we should already know about God. So, instead of lessons, we'd get to sit in the library and read all day.

Sure, the shelves were filled with religious books—but that didn't matter to me. I loved reading. I didn't care what the books were about.

128

I'd expected Vacation Bible School to be full of lectures on how to be a good Christian and avoid being a bad person. But it turned out the church was small, and Ms. Hathaway was the only person running the whole thing. So instead of lessons, we got freedom.

Every day that week, the five of us older kids lounged in big bean bags, flipping through books, reading quietly while the little kids learned Bible songs and colored pictures of Noah's Ark. It was peaceful. Honestly, it was kind of perfect.

I never told Mom about any of this, of course. If she found out I wasn't being "taught" anything, she might have said something to Ms. Hathaway—and then I'd be stuck sitting with the little kids, learning right from wrong like I was in trouble.

So, I kept it to myself and spent the week doing something I truly enjoyed: reading.

At least, until the last day.

On the last day of Vacation Bible School, Ms. Hathaway asked us older kids to help the younger ones with their art projects. The little kids had been drawing pictures and gluing macaroni onto paper to make shapes that looked like Jesus.

Our job was to set up tables outside, help the younger kids carry their projects out, and write their names on them. Ms. Hathaway explained that parents would be coming later that day to see everything their children had made during the week.

Once we finished helping, she handed each of us older kids a blank piece of paper and told us to write our names at the top, then make a list of all the books we had read that week.

So I did. I wrote Carol in big letters at the top.

See, on the first day of Bible school, when Ms. Hathaway was gathering names and sorting kids into classrooms, I told her my brother's name and my sister's name. Then, when she turned to me and asked mine, I told her Carol.

It just came out. I had been using that name for a while—it was my secret name, my new identity, and in that moment, I stuck to it.

Now, on the last day, I couldn't suddenly write my real name on the paper. That would've made things confusing. So I kept it simple and wrote Carol just like I told her.

It was only a list of books, anyway. Nothing important. Maybe no one would even notice.

All of us older kids took our papers and placed them at the very end of the table. It wasn't long before Vacation Bible School wrapped up for the week. The little kids came pouring out of the church, each one heading straight to their project and standing proudly beside it.

As the parents began arriving, the yard filled with smiling faces. Each child eagerly showed off their macaroni-and-crayon creations, and the parents beamed with pride. Afterward, the kids scattered, laughing and running around the churchyard, free to play.

Ms. Hathaway did her best to speak to every parent, thanking them for sending their kids and talking about how much fun the week had been.

I noticed Mom standing by Michael's project. She and Ms. Hathaway were deep in conversation, laughing and talking about how smart Michael was and how creative his project looked. Then Mom slowly made her way to Mia's table. Same thing—compliments, smiles, and talk about how sweet and shy Mia was.

I quietly slipped away, hoping that if I ran around the yard with the other kids, Mom might forget to look for my paper.

I kept glancing back, watching nervously as Mom and Ms. Hathaway chatted. I crossed my fingers that Mom would decide it was time to leave, without checking my list. Because on that paper, in big bold letters, was the name Carol.

Ms. Hathaway didn't know my real name. And Mom didn't know I'd been using a fake one all week.

Then, just like I feared, Mom wandered over to the end of the table—the one with the reading lists. I watched as she scanned each paper, her face slowly shifting from curious to confused. She couldn't find my name.

She waved Ms. Hathaway over, interrupting her conversation with another parent. I saw her pointing toward me as I pretended to run and play with the little kids.

Ms. Hathaway said something, and then Mom turned, locked eyes with me, and hollered, "Get over here. Now."

My heart sank.

The moment had come. The gig was up.

When I reached them, Ms. Hathaway asked, "Why did you tell me your name was Carol?"

Right behind her, Mom echoed the question—sharper this time: "Why did you tell Ms. Hathaway your name was Carol?"

I had no answer. I stood frozen in silence, the weight of the moment too heavy for words. Mom offered a quiet apology to Ms. Hathaway, then turned to me and said curtly, "Go get your brother and sister."

We walked home without a word. Each step felt heavier than the last. That walk—short as it was—felt like it stretched for miles.

Back at the trailer, Mom didn't yell. She didn't even look at me. She just pointed to the steps and said, "Sit outside until your father gets home."

And that's when the real punishment began.

The waiting.

There's a particular kind of fear that only comes when you're a kid waiting for your dad to come home and find out what you've done. The kind that makes your chest tight and your thoughts run in circles.

I sat there on those steps while the sun inched across the sky, every second like a drumbeat inside my head. I imagined his face, the sound of his voice, the shame he'd feel that I'd embarrassed the family—changed my name like I didn't want to belong.

I waited for hours, stewing in guilt, sweat clinging to my skin, stomach churning with every crunch of gravel that wasn't him. I was sure I'd ruined everything. That I'd be grounded for life, that maybe he'd yell. Or worse—be disappointed.

Then I heard the engine.

His truck pulled in, dust kicking up behind him.

I stood quickly, heart racing. I wiped my face, pulled my shoulders back, and braced myself for what was coming.

But it didn't come.

He barely looked at me.

"Tiny!" he shouted, already halfway to the door. "Pack it up! We're moving again—Wyoming this time!"

And just like that, life changed.

Mom appeared, stunned. He rattled off details: leave by morning, everything packed tonight and still had to tell the rest of the crew.

Then he was gone again, back down the road, off to spread the news.

Mom stared after him for a second, then turned to me and said, "Well? Don't just stand there. Get in here and help me pack."

That was it.

No lecture. No punishment. No mention of what I'd done. The hours I spent sweating on those steps were swallowed up in an instant by the urgency of packing.

I never got to explain myself. Never got to tell Ms. Hathaway I was sorry. Never had to face Harold and tell him that Carol wasn't my real name (although something told me that Harold probably wouldn't care). I never told any of the other kids my real name either. Some of those kids would continue moving with us while others I would never see again, like Mario and his little brother. Everything I had become, the good and the bad, was gone within minutes. And that's how it would be for the next few years. Every time we moved it would be a surprise from Dad. We wouldn't get to say goodbye to new friends or neighbors or anyone. We would just leave in the early morning hours and watch the town disappear in the rearview mirror.

Moving to Duchesne, Utah, felt like stepping into an entirely new world. We were there for just four months, but each day brought new and different things. And then, out of the blue, we were moving again—this time to Cheyenne, Wyoming.

All the moving would teach me one thing above all: no one stays around for long. It was like every place we went, everyone we met, was temporary. In Duchesne, Utah, I learned how quickly people could come and go, like fleeting shadows.

Then we moved to Cheyenne, Wyoming, and I started the cycle all over again—another new beginning, another chance to start fresh, but in the end, nothing lasting ever really took root.

Years later, when we finally did settled down, I thought things would be different. But the truth was, all the years of moving, of seeing people drift in and out of my life, would make it hard to hold on to anything permanent. I couldn't seem to build lasting relationships, no matter how much I tried. It was as if I'd conditioned myself to expect that people would leave, or that I would have to leave them. The habit of letting go became a part of me. And in the end, that's what I carried with me—more distance than connection. It was a hard habit to unlearn.

www.ingramcontent.com/pod-product-compliance
Lightning Source LLC
Chambersburg PA
CBHW050443150626
46551CB00028B/1168